ZAGZIG SERIES
Directed by
PHILIPPE LANGLOIS & FRANK SMITH

IN THE SAME SERIES

LAURIE ANDERSON: *NOTHING IN MY POCKETS*
JONAS MEKAS: *TO PETRARCA*
LEAH SINGER & LEE RANALDO: *WATER DAYS*
WINTER FAMILY: *NO WORLD*
RYOJI IKEDA: *DATAPHONICS*
GISELE VIENNE, DENNIS COOPER, PETER REHBERG: *JERK*
CHLOE: *CHASSER CROISER*
SOUNDWALK COLLECTIVE: *MEDEA*
CHRISTIAN MARCLAY: *FIRE & WATER*
LORIS GREAUD: *CROSSFADING*
VANESSA PLACE: *LAST WORD*

www.disvoir.com

ISBN 978-2-914563-51-2

Audio CD offered n°133938 ZagZig004 © Ryoji Ikeda
The sound piece *Dataphonics* (60') was commissioned by the Atelier de Création Radiophonique (ACR) de France Culture, with the support of the Centre national des arts plastiques (CNAP) and the Ministère de la culture et de la communication, as part of a public commission. It was broadcast on September 2, 2007. www.franceculture.com

Printed with help of

Région IledeFrance

dataphonics

Ryoji Ikeda

dataphonics	track name	interval [mm:ss]	channel [left/right]

0 — 1200 / 44100 sec

dataphonics [2006-07] is a music project by ryoji ikeda, which focuses on the relationship between the sound of data and the data of sound. It spans various formats - multi-channel sound performance, radio broadcasts and audio/data research.

dataphonics [radio series] was commissioned by L'Atelier de Création Radiophonique de France Culture. It consists of ten six-minute segments, first broadcast monthly on Radio France during 2006-07. Various non-audio data were converted forcefully to audio data, which became the materials from which the tracks were composed. Moreover, this book examines the visualization of the composed tracks through the ultimate binary reduction of sound waveforms.

dataphonics forms part of datamatics, an ongoing project by ryoji ikeda since 2006, in which he explores the potential to perceive the invisible multi-substance of data that permeates our world through audiovisual concerts, installations, cds and publications.

design & programming: Tomonaga Tokuyama

binary conversion of sound waveform

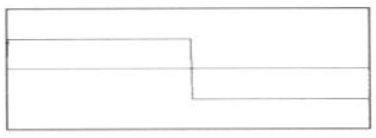

waveform 1

binary code 1

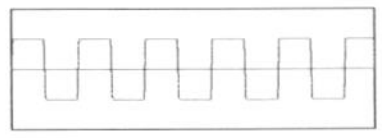

waveform 2

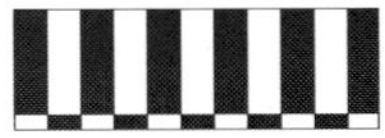

binary code 2

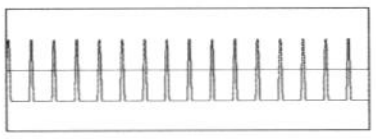

waveform 3

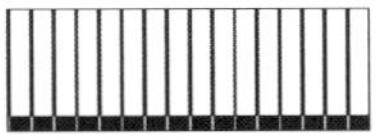

binary code 3

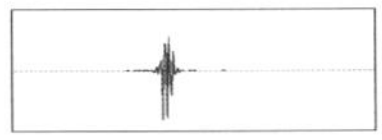

waveform 4

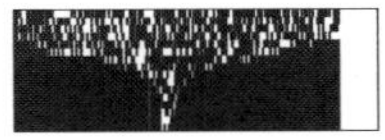

binary code 4

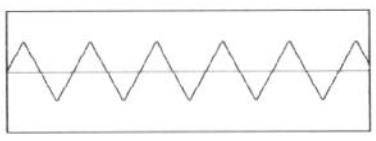

waveform 5

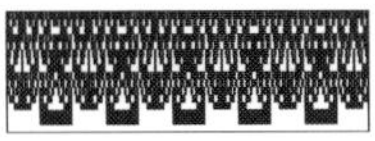

binary code 5

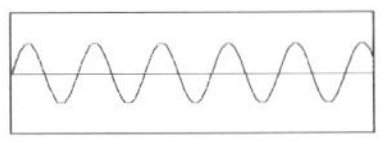

waveform 6

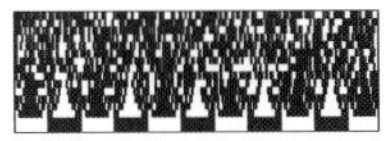

binary code 6

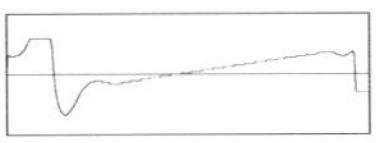

waveform 7

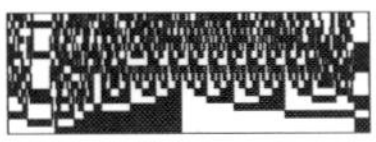

binary code 7

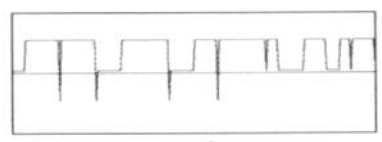

waveform 8

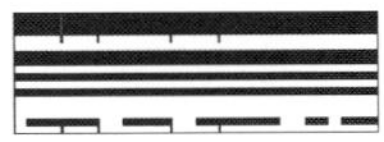

binary code 8

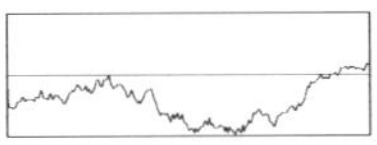

waveform 9

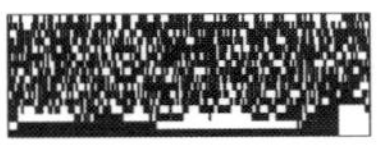

binary code 9

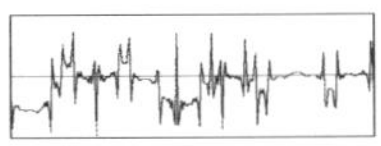

waveform 10

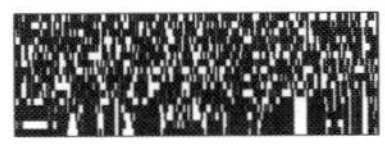

binary code 10

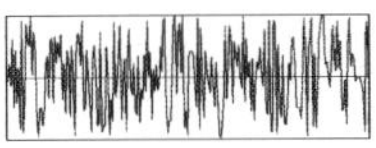

waveform 11

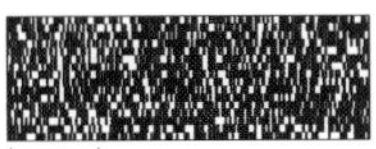

binary code 11

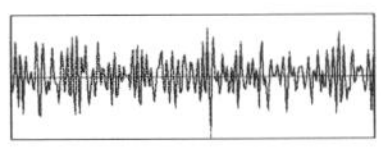

waveform 12

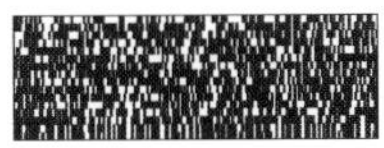

binary code 12

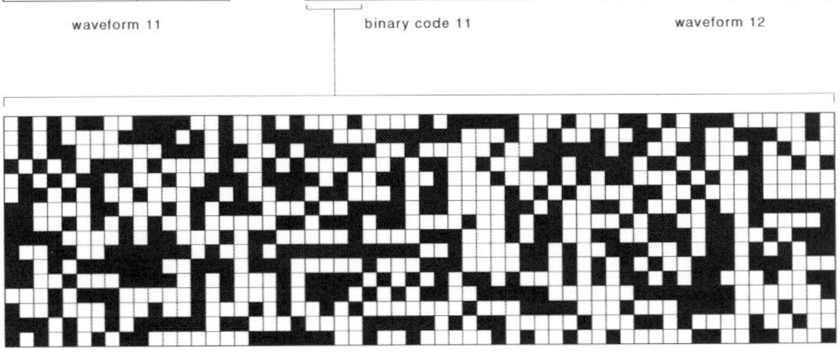

0	1	0	1	0	1	1	0	0	1	1	1	1	0	0	1	0	0	1	0	1	0	0	0	1	0	0	0	0	1	0	1	1	1	1	1	0	0	0	1	0	0	0	1	1	0	1	0	1	1	1	0	0	0	0	0	1	0	0x0001	LSB
0	1	0	1	0	0	0	0	1	1	1	1	0	1	0	1	0	0	1	1	1	1	1	0	0	0	1	1	1	1	1	1	0	0	0	1	0	0	1	0	0	1	0	0	1	1	0	0	1	0	0	1	1	1	0	0	1	0	0x0002	
0	1	0	1	1	0	0	0	0	0	0	1	1	1	0	1	1	0	0	1	0	1	1	1	1	1	0	0	1	0	0	0	0	0	1	0	0	1	1	1	1	1	0	1	1	0	0	1	1	0	0	0	1	0	1	0	0	0	0x0004	
1	0	1	0	1	0	1	1	1	0	1	0	0	0	0	1	0	0	1	0	1	0	0	0	1	0	0	1	0	1	1	0	0	1	0	0	1	1	1	0	1	1	1	1	0	1	1	0	1	0	0	1	1	0	0	1	0	1	0x0008	
0	1	0	1	0	1	1	0	1	0	0	1	0	0	1	1	1	0	1	1	1	1	0	1	0	0	1	1	0	0	1	0	0	0	1	0	0	0	1	0	1	0	1	1	0	0	0	1	0	1	0	0	1	0	0	0	0	0	0x0010	
0	1	1	0	1	0	1	0	0	1	0	0	0	1	1	0	1	0	0	1	1	0	1	1	0	0	0	1	0	1	1	0	0	0	0	1	0	1	0	1	0	0	0	0	1	1	0	0	1	0	0	0	1	0	0	0	0	0	0x0020	
1	1	0	0	0	0	1	1	0	0	0	1	0	1	0	1	1	1	0	0	0	1	0	0	1	1	1	1	0	1	1	0	0	0	0	1	1	0	1	0	0	1	1	0	1	0	0	1	0	1	0	0	1	1	1	1	1	1	0x0040	
1	1	0	0	1	0	1	0	1	0	1	0	0	1	0	0	0	0	0	1	1	0	1	1	1	0	1	1	0	0	0	0	1	0	0	1	0	1	1	0	0	0	0	1	0	1	1	0	0	1	1	0	1	0	0	0	0	1	0x0080	
1	1	1	1	0	0	0	0	1	0	1	1	0	0	0	1	0	1	1	0	0	0	0	0	1	0	0	0	0	1	1	1	0	0	0	1	0	1	1	0	0	1	1	0	0	1	1	1	0	1	1	0	0	1	0	1	1	1	0x0100	MSB
1	0	0	1	1	0	0	1	1	1	1	1	1	0	1	0	0	1	0	1	1	1	1	1	1	1	1	1	1	0	0	1	0	0	0	0	1	1	0	1	0	0	1	1	1	0	0	1	0	1	1	0	1	0	1	0	1	1	0x0200	
1	1	0	1	0	1	1	1	1	1	1	0	0	1	1	1	0	1	1	1	0	0	0	0	0	1	0	0	0	1	1	1	0	0	0	0	1	1	0	1	0	1	0	1	0	1	0	0	1	1	1	0	1	1	1	0	0	0	0x0400	
1	1	0	0	1	0	0	0	1	1	1	1	0	1	0	1	0	0	0	1	0	1	1	1	1	0	1	0	1	0	1	0	1	1	0	1	0	0	0	1	0	1	0	1	1	0	1	0	1	1	0	0	0	1	0	0	1	1	0x0800	
0	0	0	1	0	1	1	1	0	0	0	0	0	1	0	1	0	0	0	1	0	1	1	1	0	1	0	1	0	1	1	0	0	1	1	1	1	1	0	0	0	0	0	0	1	1	1	1	1	1	1	0	0	0	0	0	0	1	0x1000	
1	0	0	1	0	0	0	1	0	0	1	0	0	1	0	0	0	1	0	1	0	0	1	0	1	0	0	0	0	0	0	0	1	0	0	0	1	1	1	1	0	0	0	1	0	0	0	1	1	1	1	0	0	0	1	0	0	0	0x2000	
1	1	1	0	1	0	0	1	0	1	1	1	1	1	0	1	1	0	0	0	1	0	0	0	0	1	1	1	1	1	0	1	0	1	1	0	0	0	0	0	1	0	0	0	1	1	0	1	0	0	0	0	1	0	0	1	0	0	0x4000	
1	0	1	0	1	0	1	0	1	1	0	0	0	0	0	0	0	1	1	1	1	1	1	0	0	1	0	0	1	0	0	0	0	0	1	0	1	0	0	1	0	0	1	0	0	0	0	0	1	1	0	0	1	1	0	0	0	1	sign bit	

dataphonics 01 principle 00:00 - 02:00 left

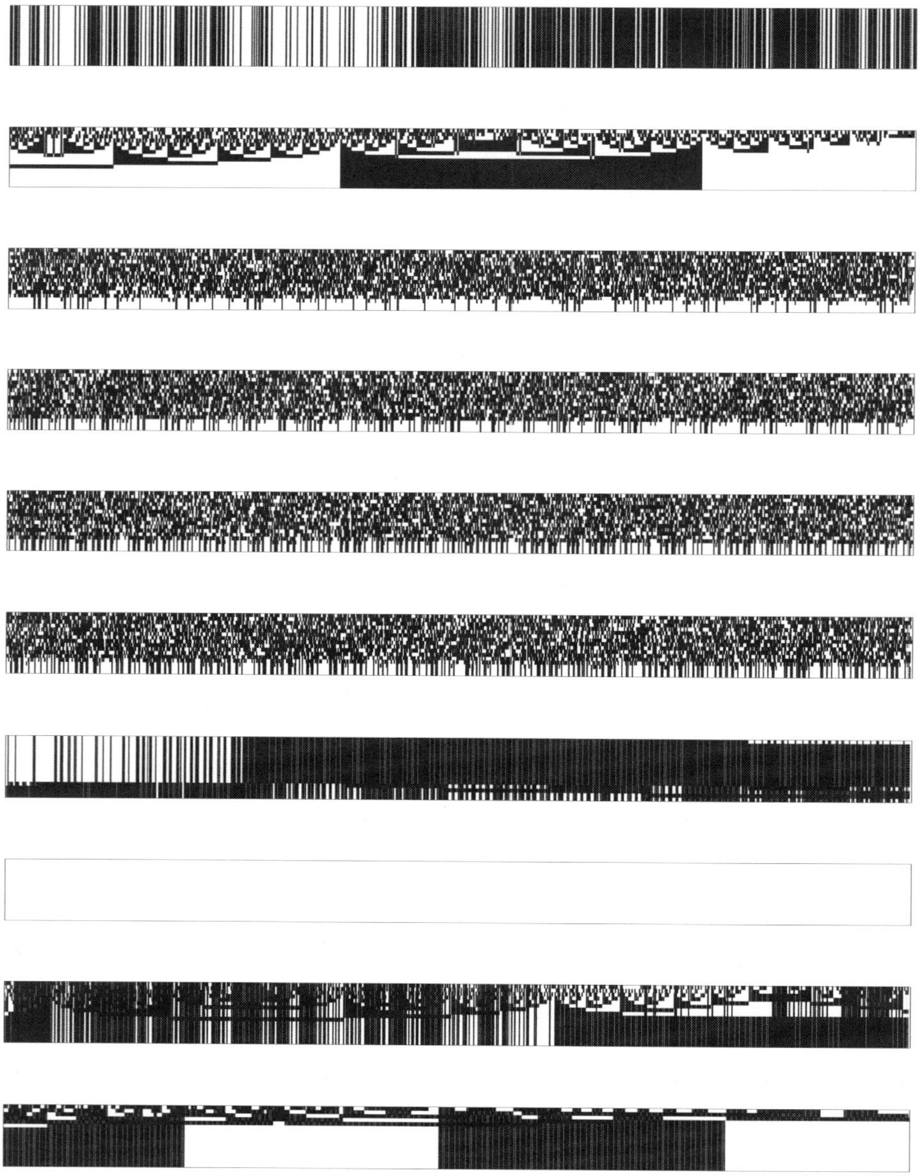

dataphonics 01 principle 00:00 - 02:00 right

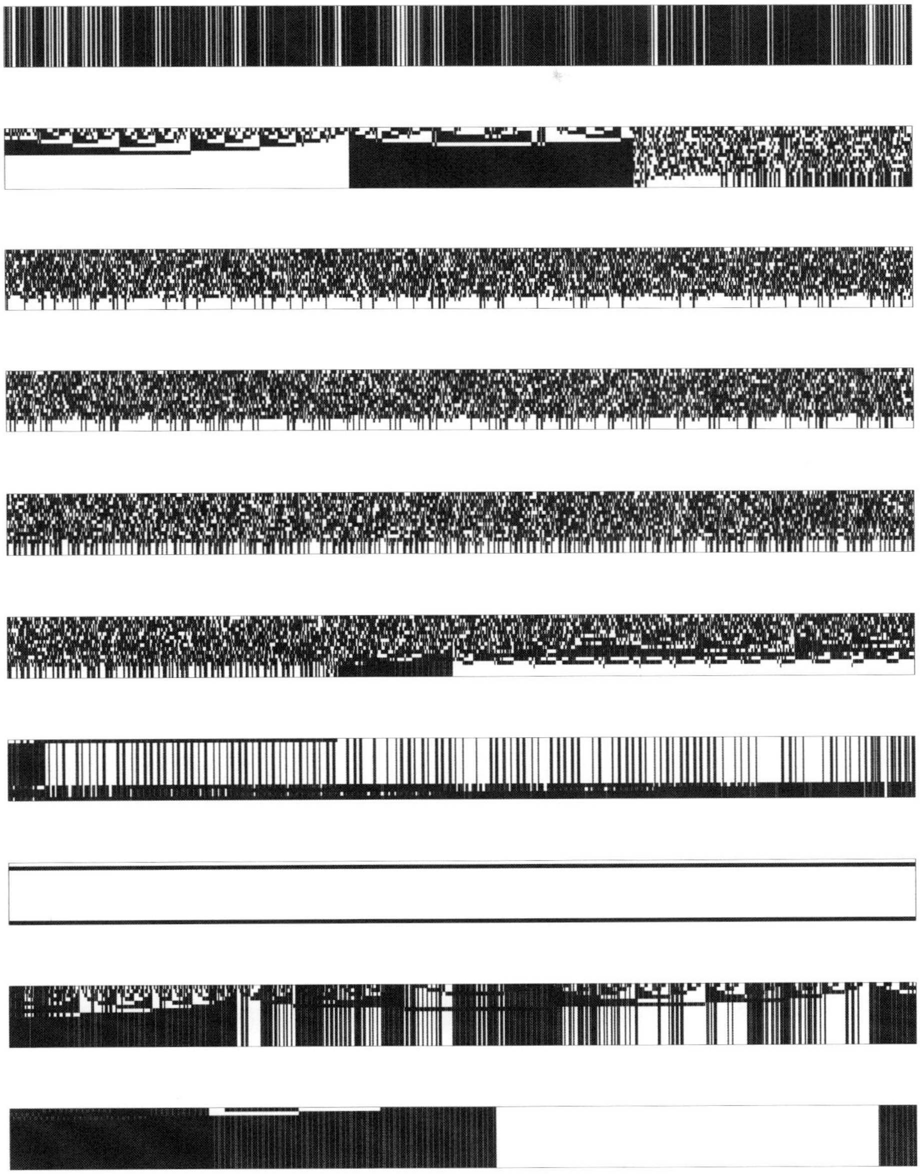

dataphonics 01 principle 02:00 - 04:00 left

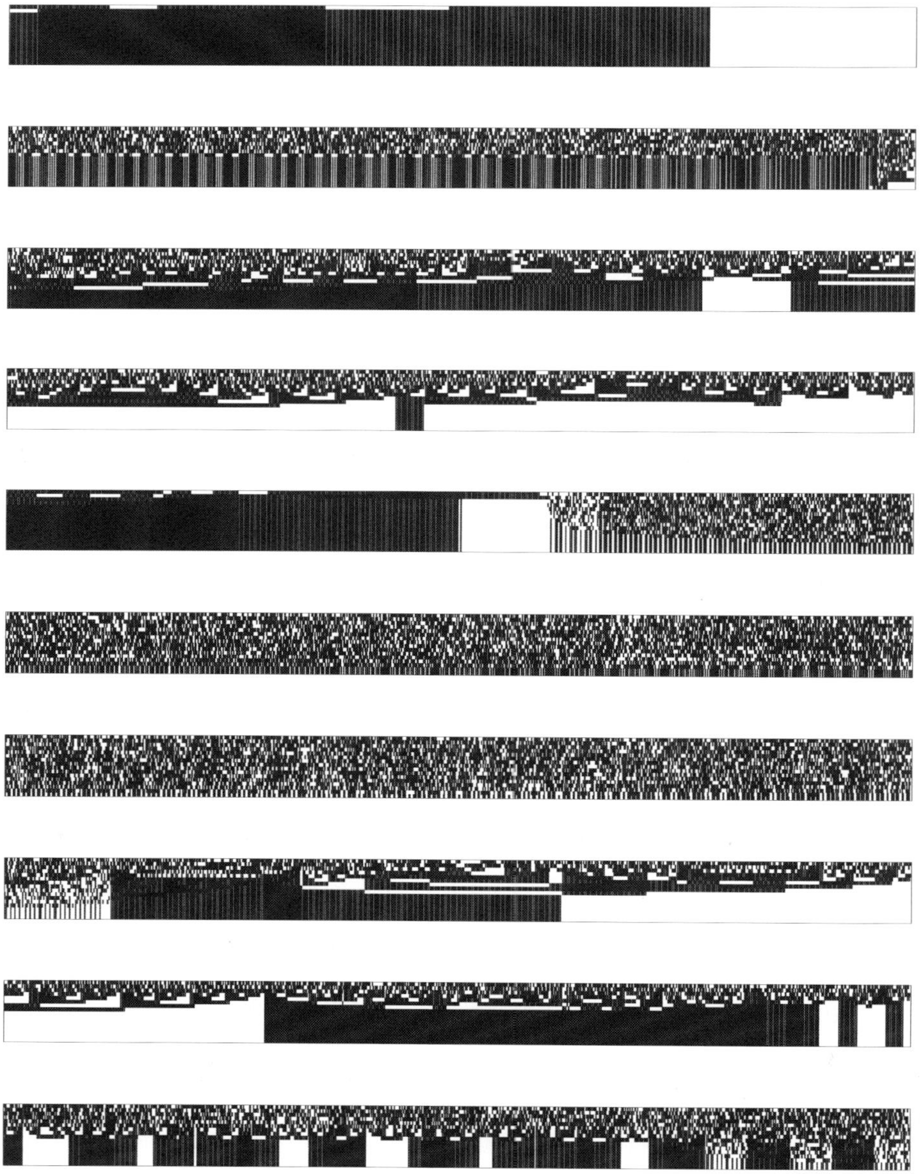

dataphonics 01 principle 02:00 - 04:00 right

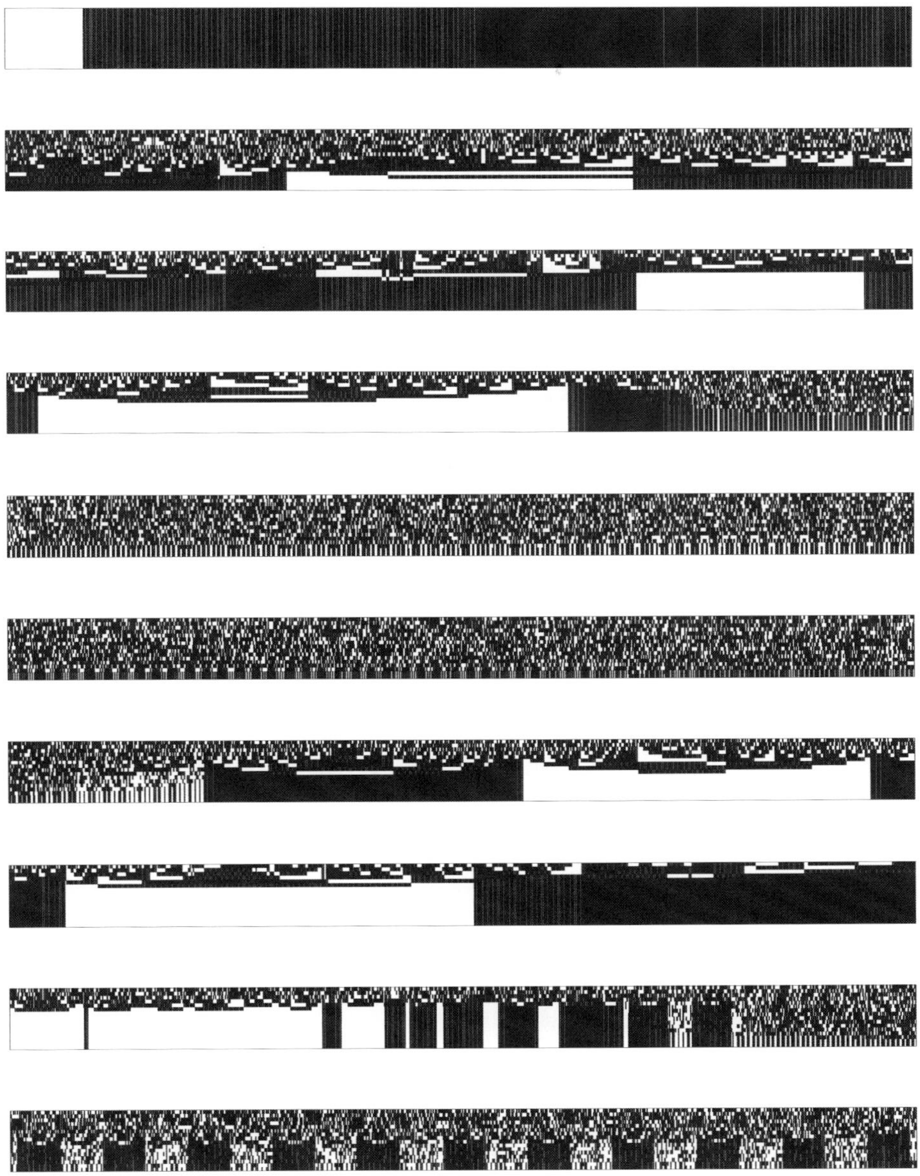

dataphonics 01 principle 04:00 - 06:00 left

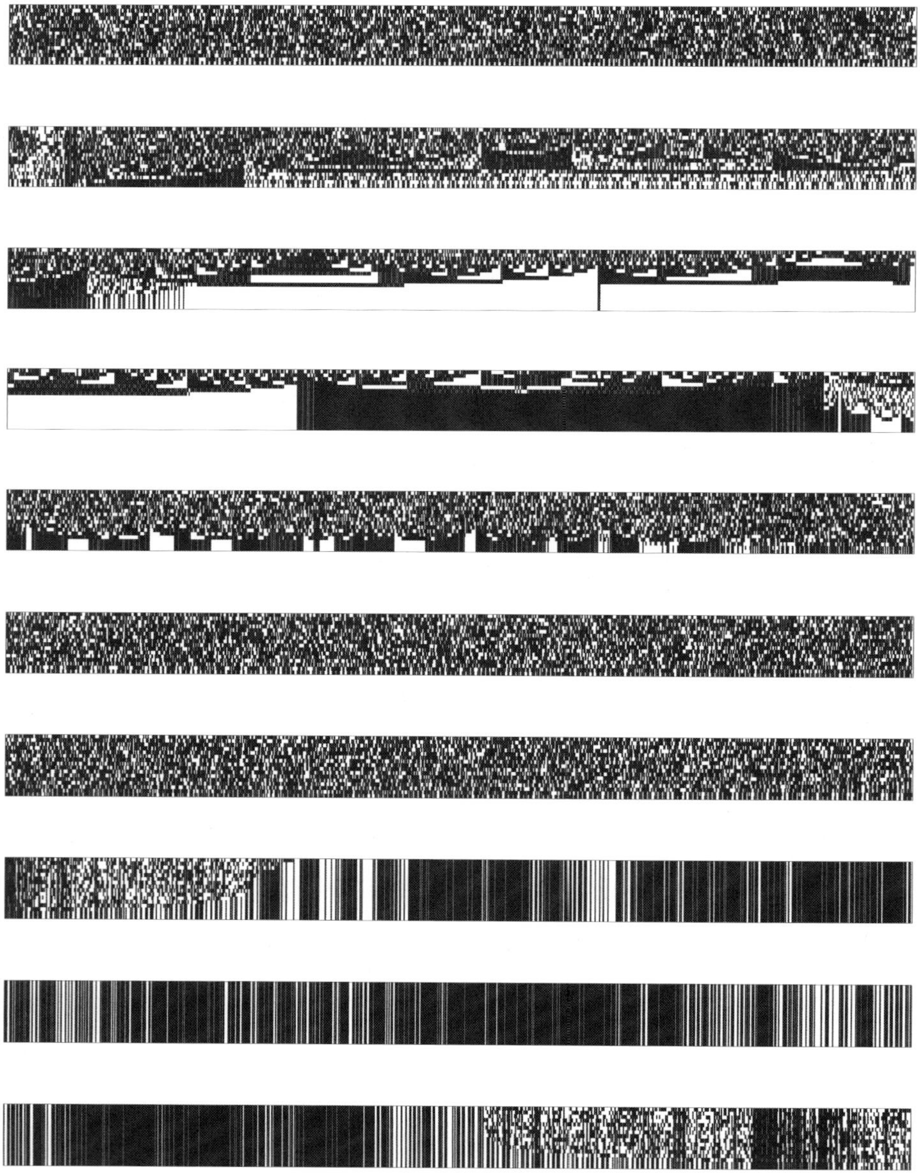

dataphonics 01 principle 04:00 - 06:00 right

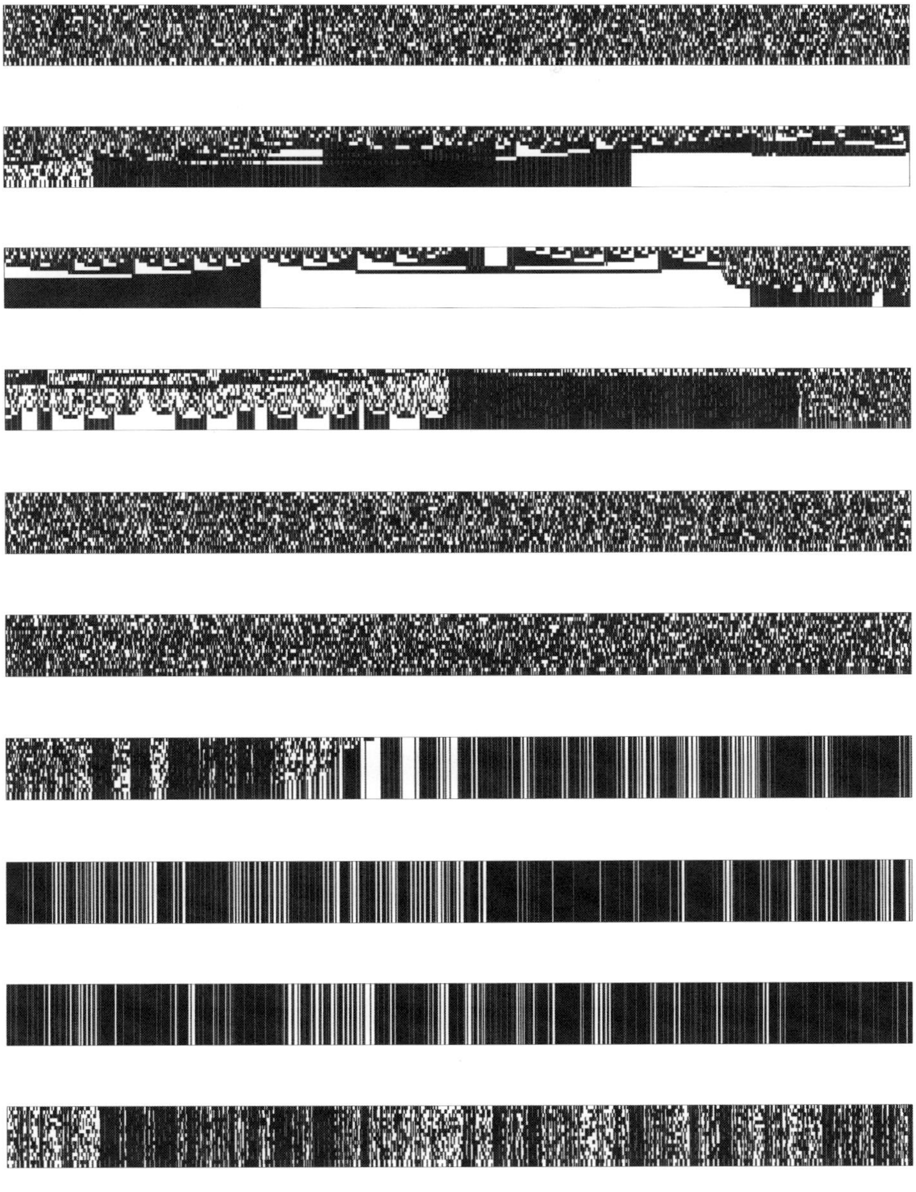

dataphonics 02 spectrum 00:00 - 03:00 left

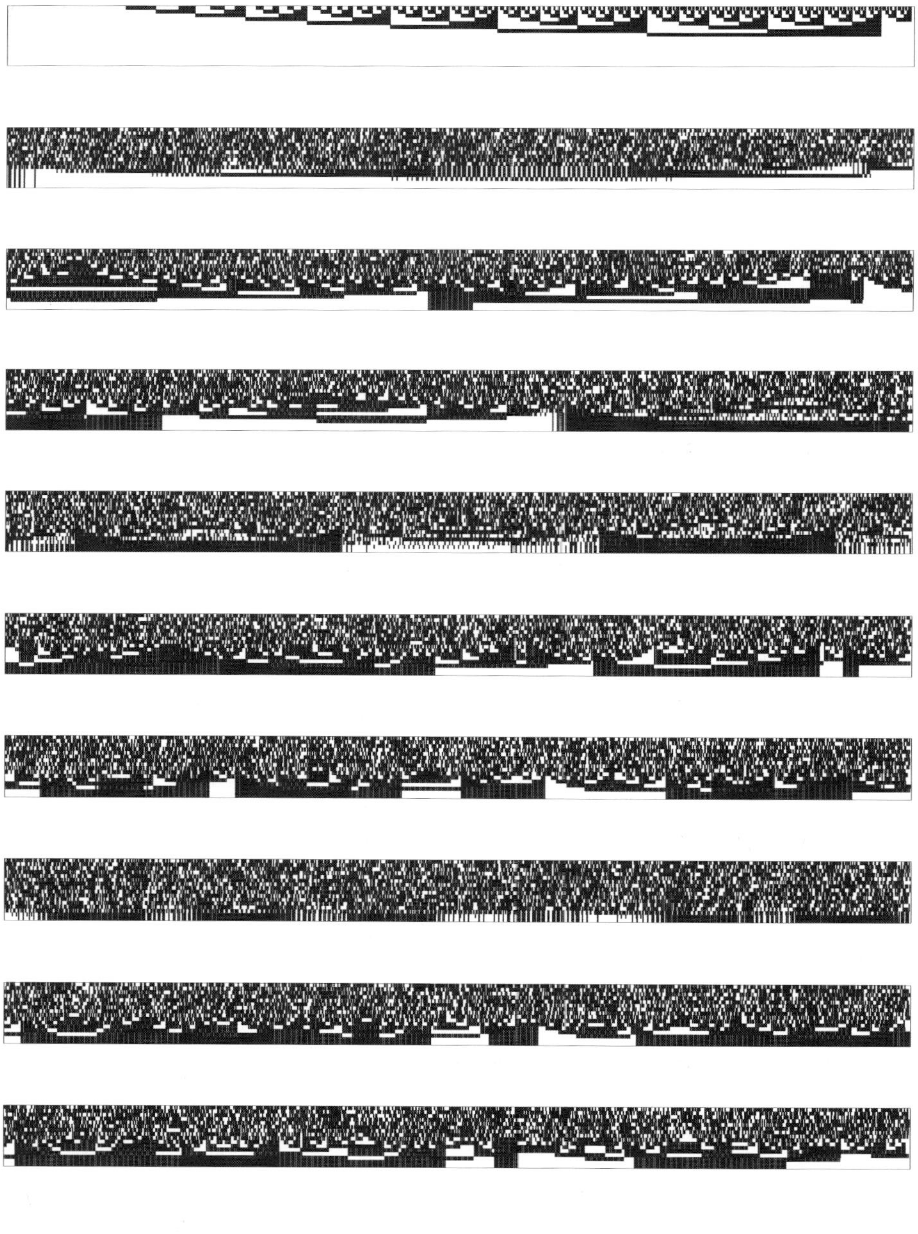

dataphonics 02 spectrum 00:00 - 03:00 right

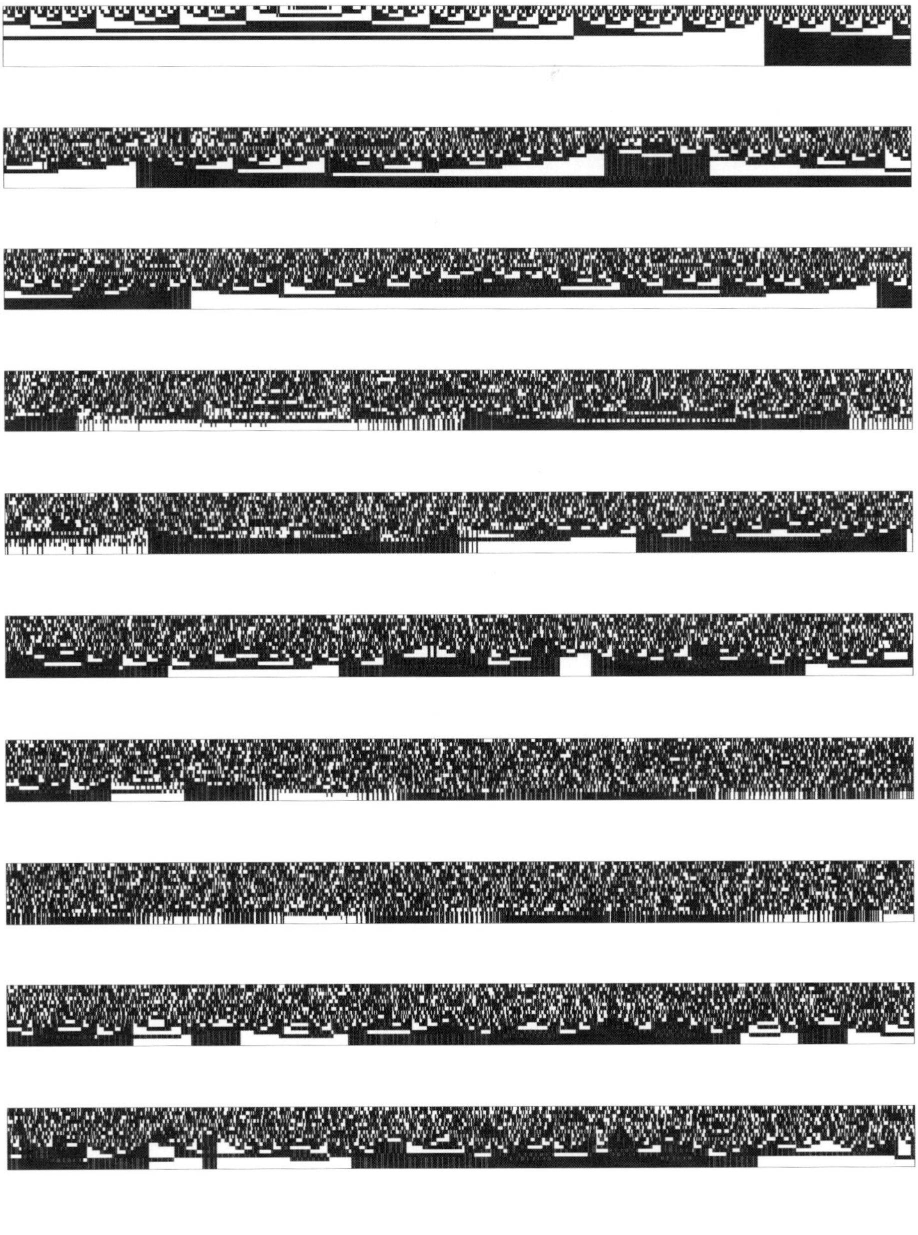

dataphonics 02 spectrum 03:00 - 06:00 left

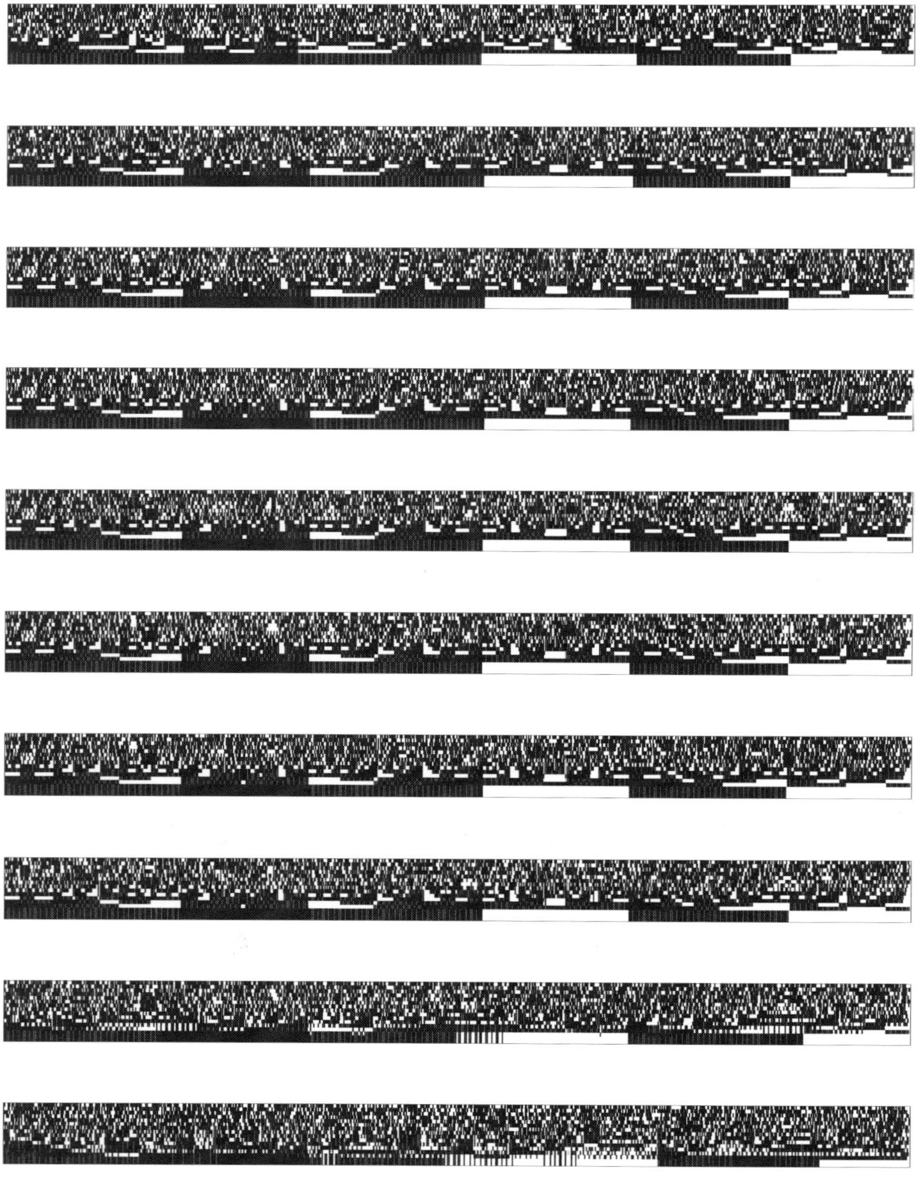

dataphonics 02 spectrum 03:00 - 06:00 right

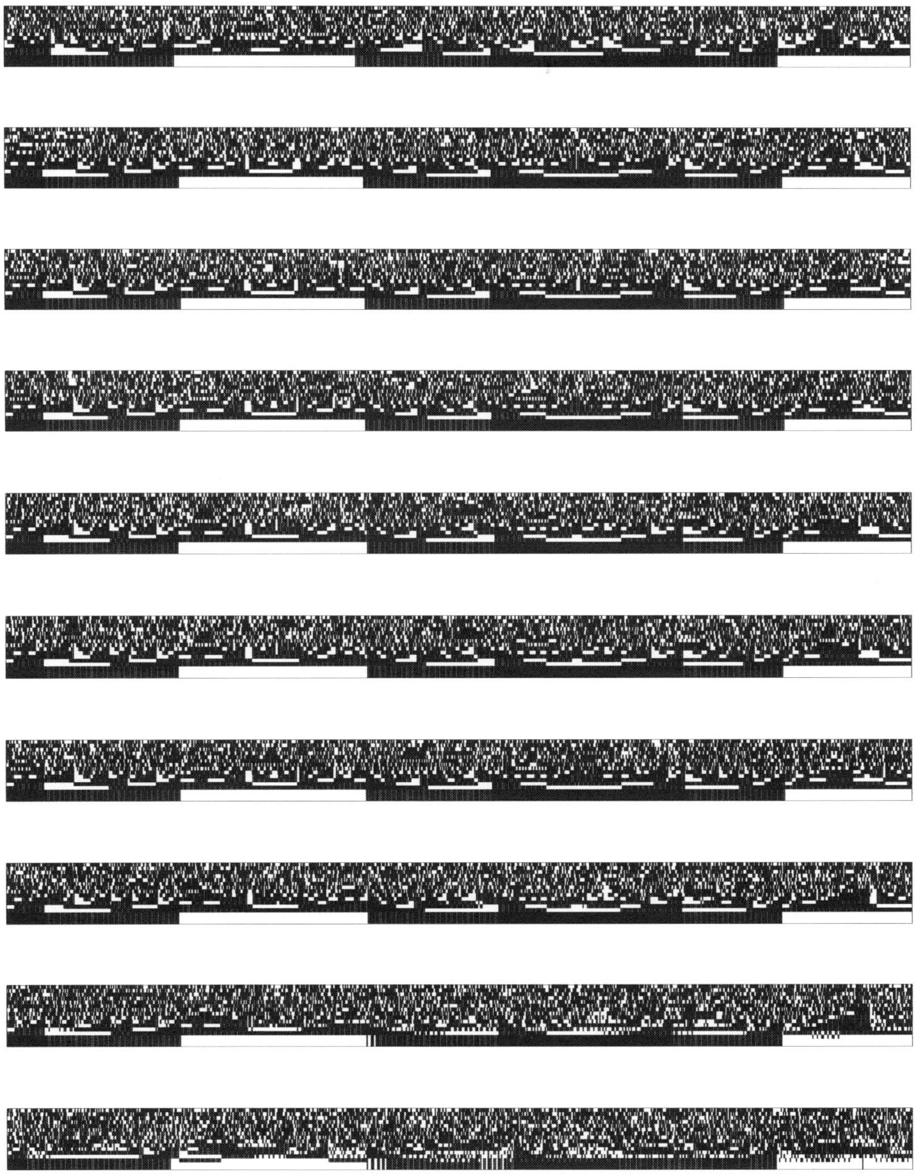

dataphonics 03 transmission 00:00 - 02:00 left

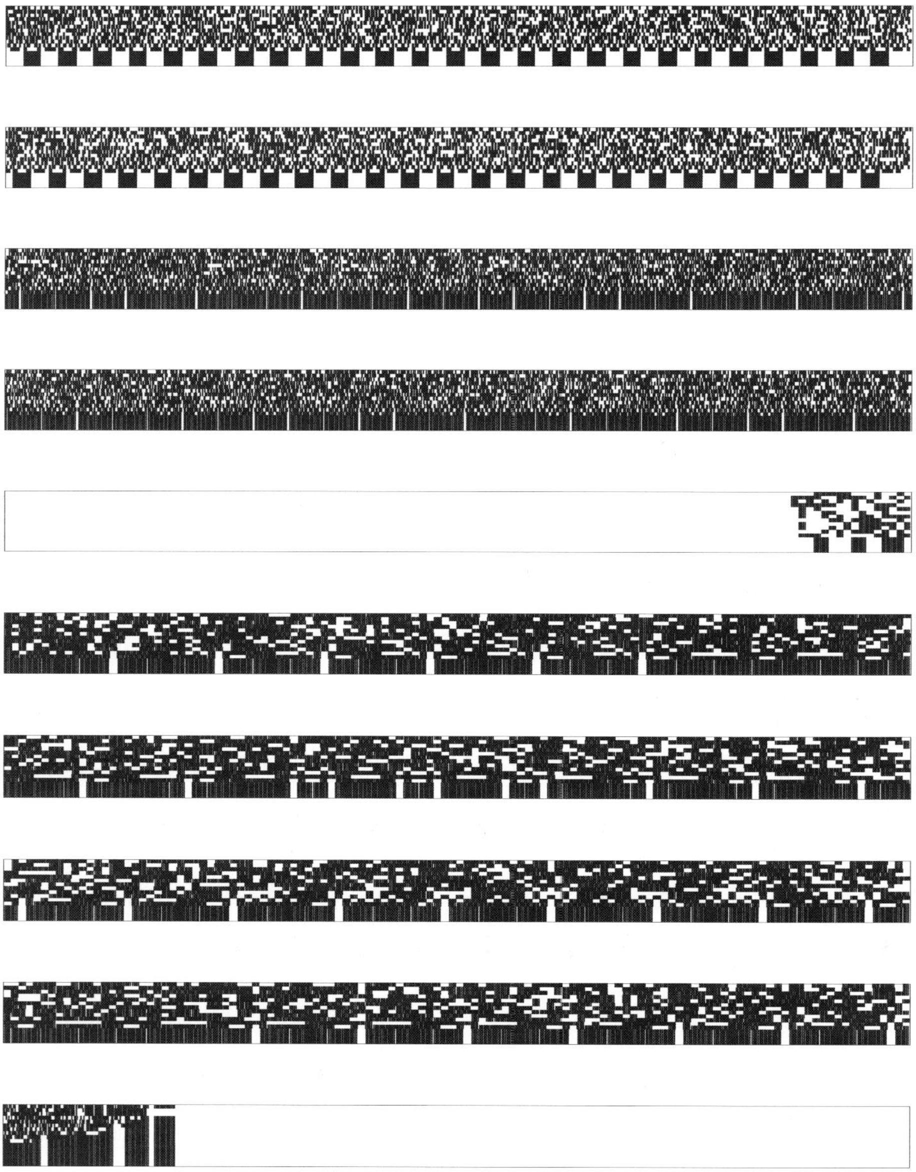

dataphonics 03 transmission 00:00 - 02:00 right

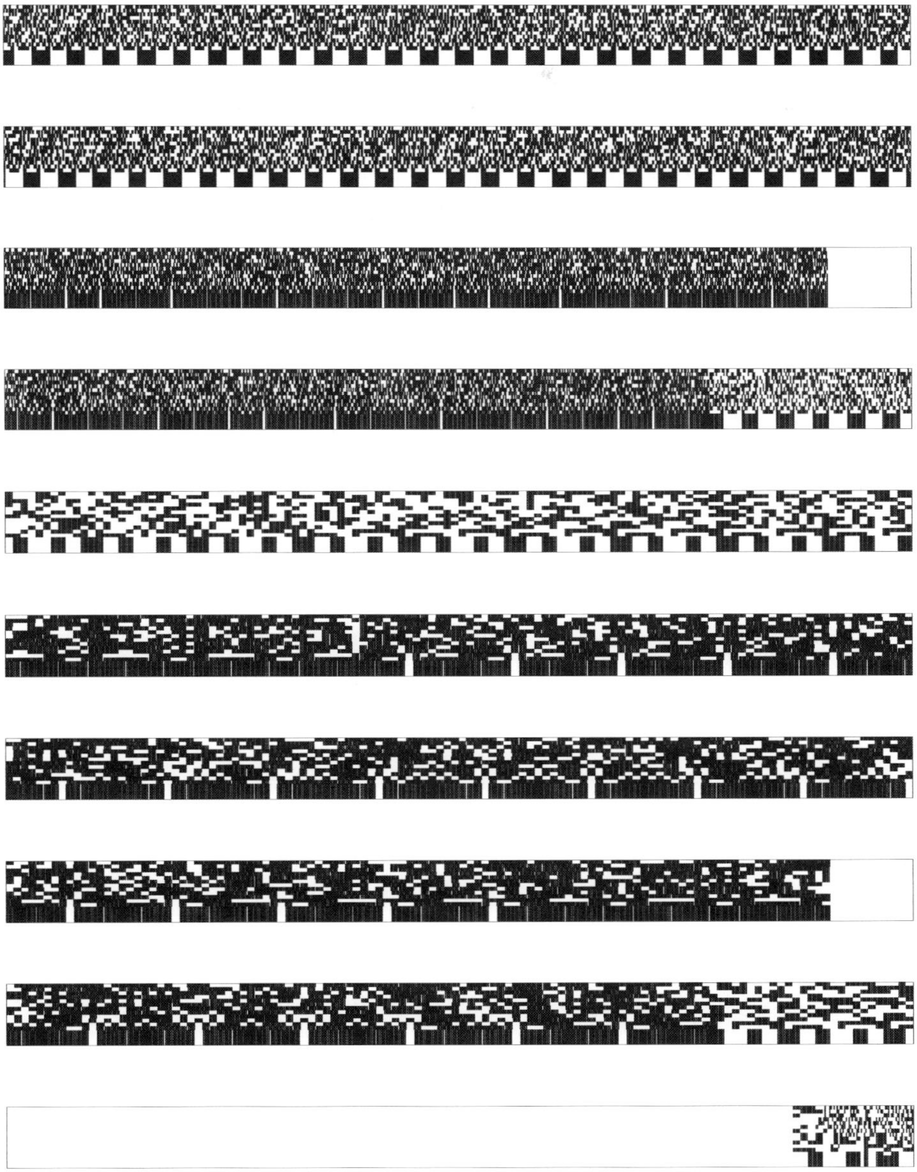

dataphonics 03 transmission 02:00 - 04:00 left

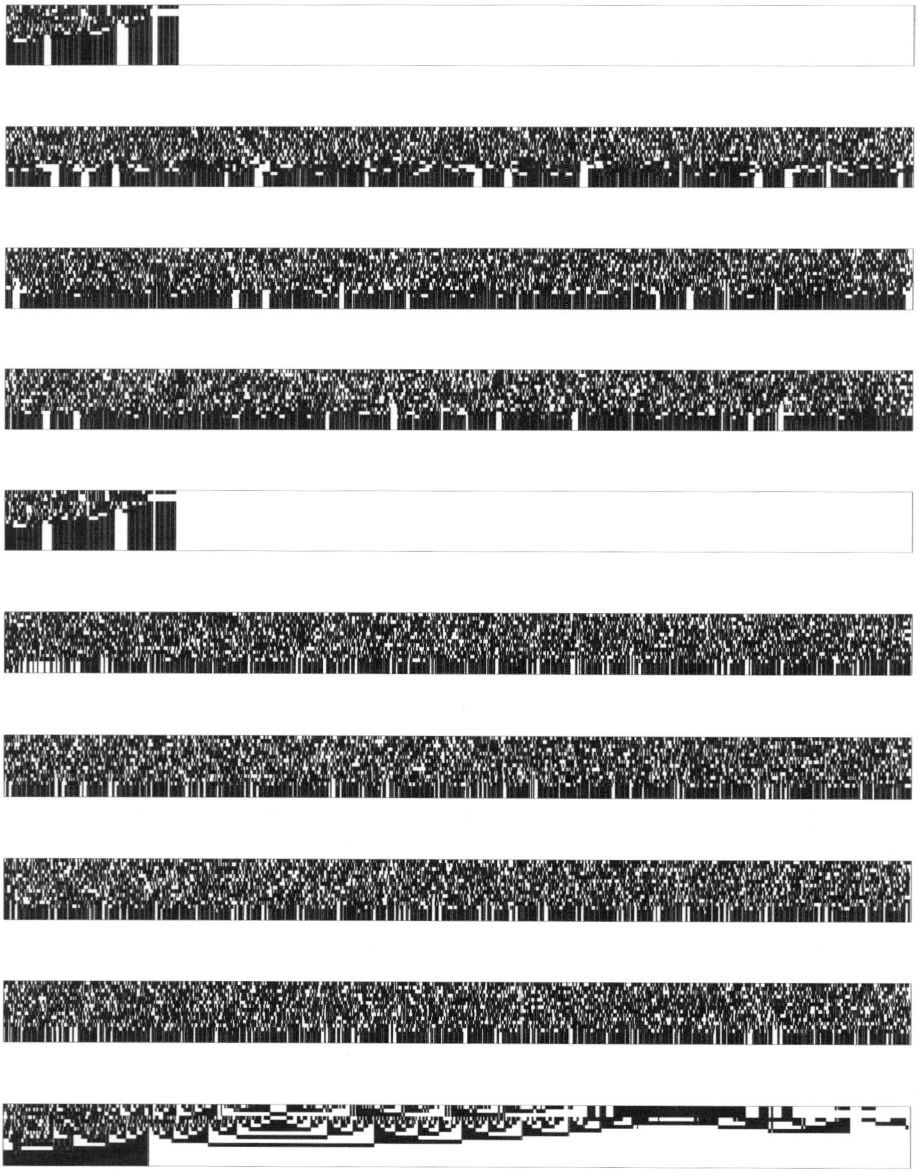

dataphonics 03 transmission 02:00 - 04:00 right

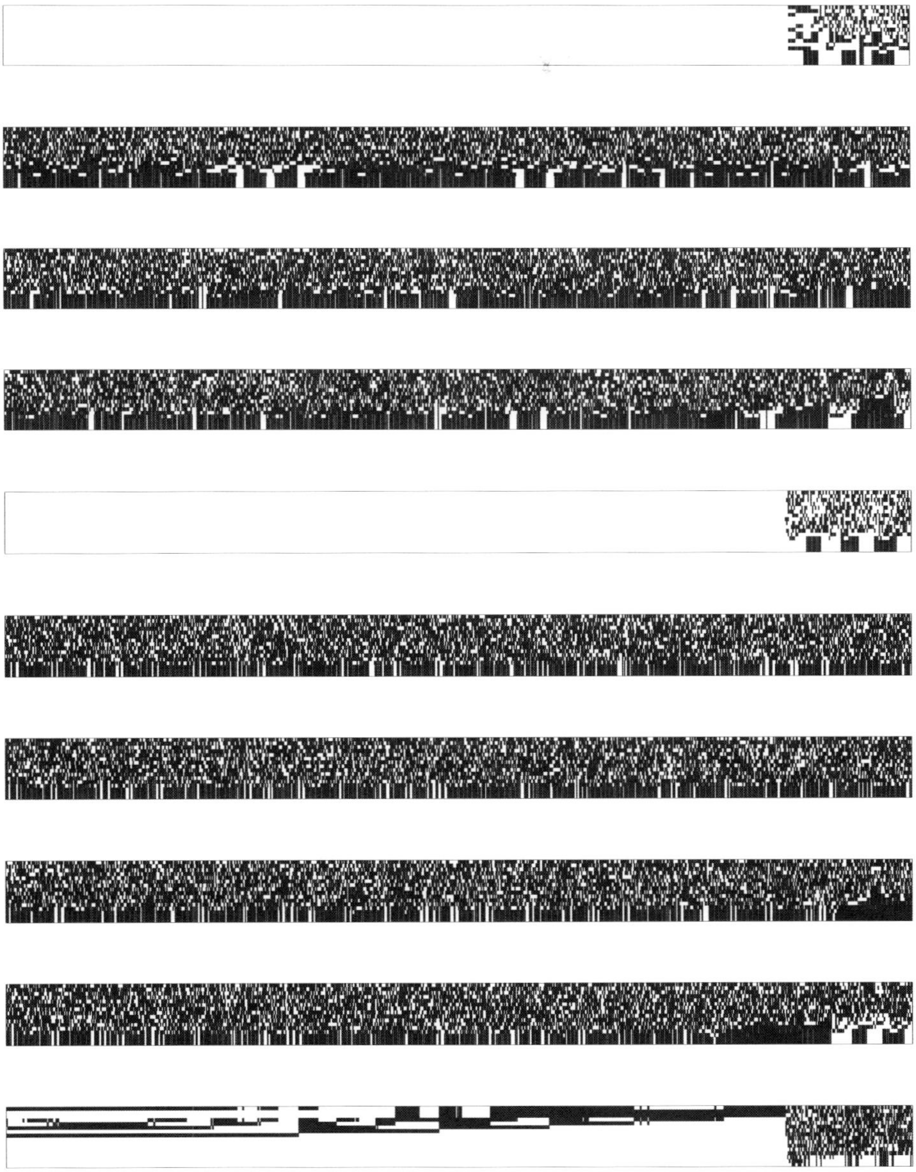

dataphonics 03 transmission 04:00 - 06 00 left

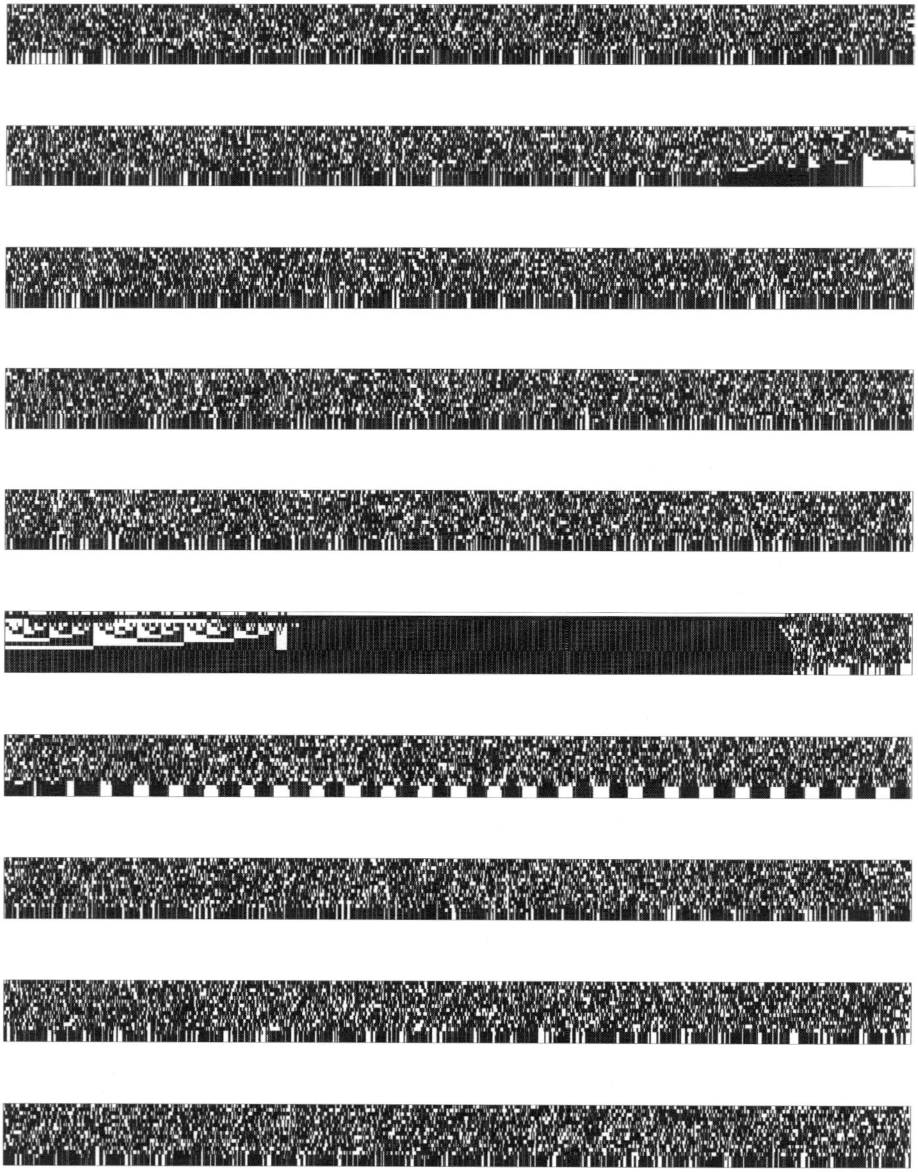

dataphonics 03 transmission 04:00 - 06:00 right

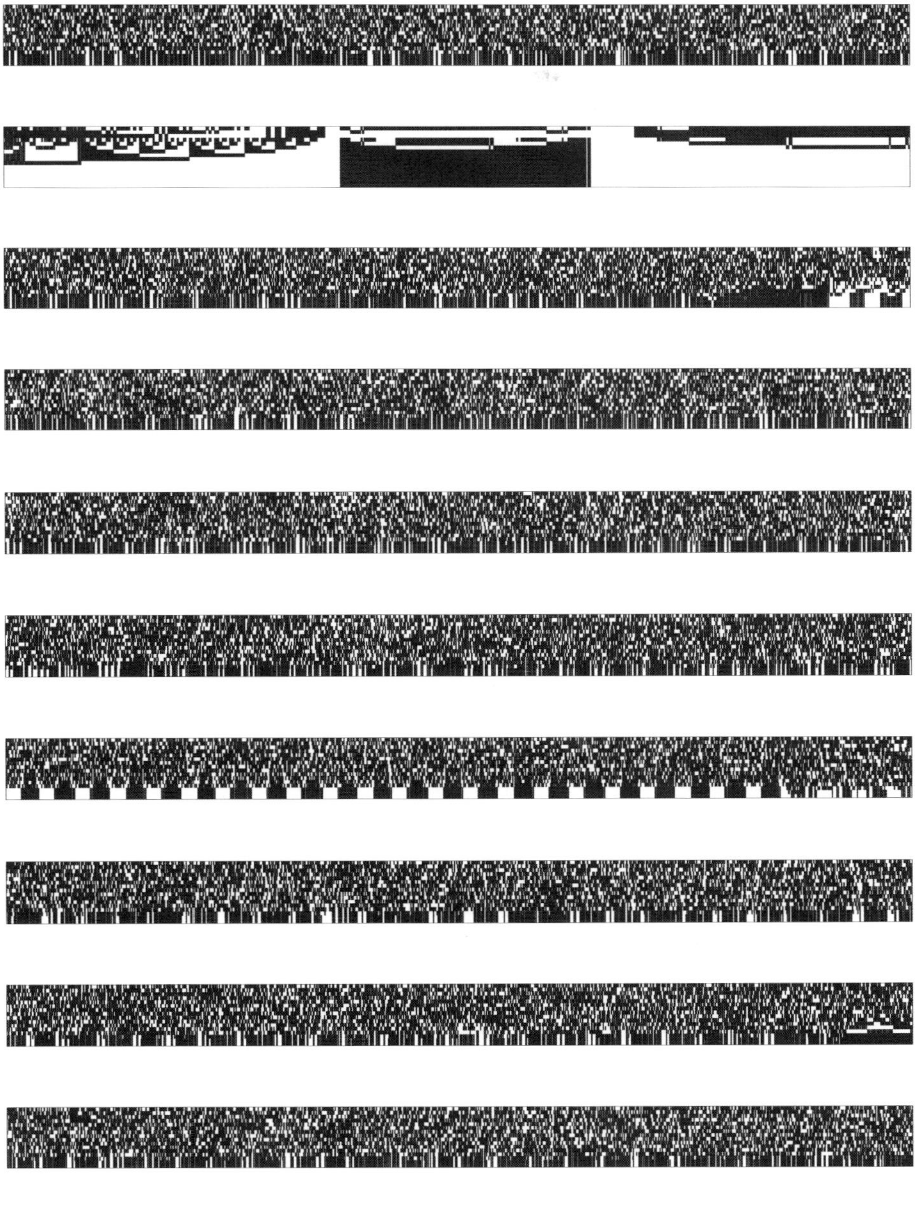

dataphonics 04 transformation 00:00 - 02:00 left

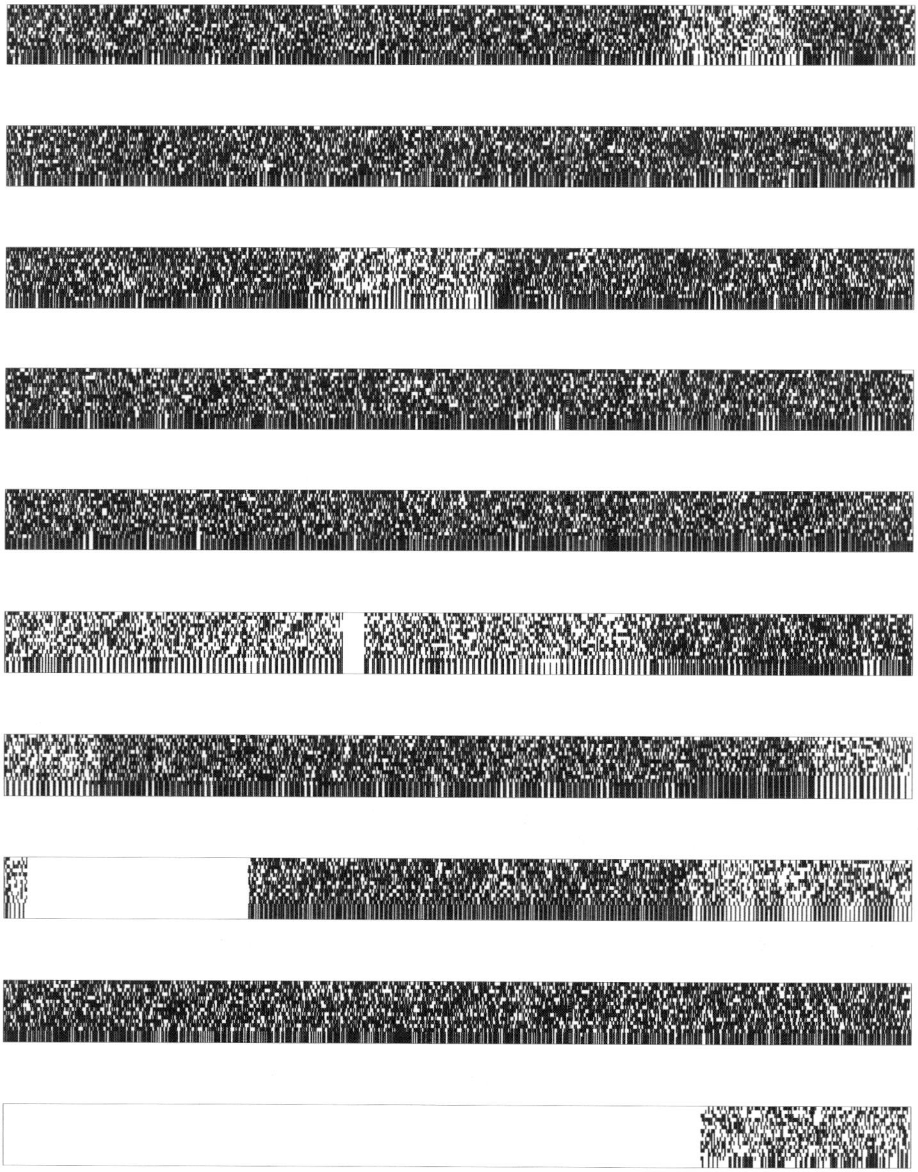

dataphonics 04 transformation 00:00 - 02:00 right

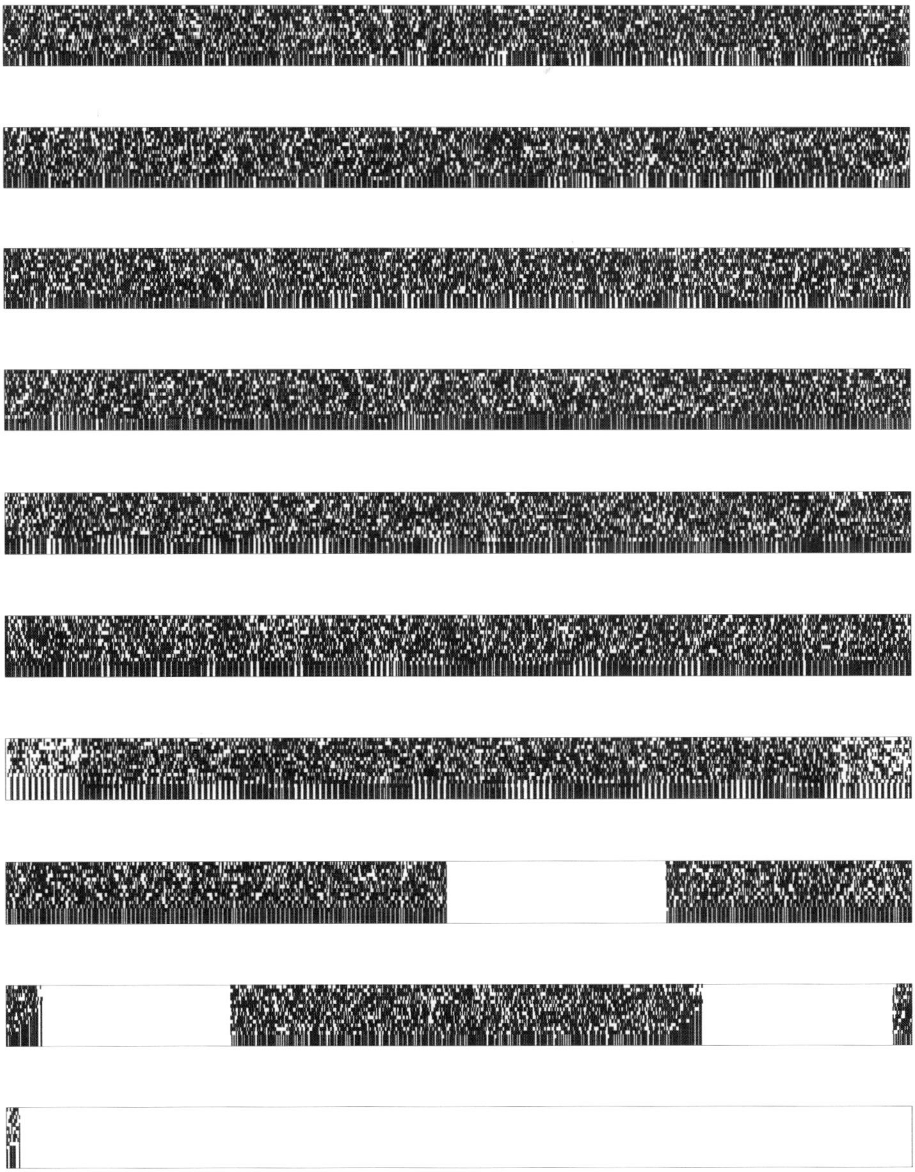

dataphonics 04 transformation 02:00 - 04:00 left

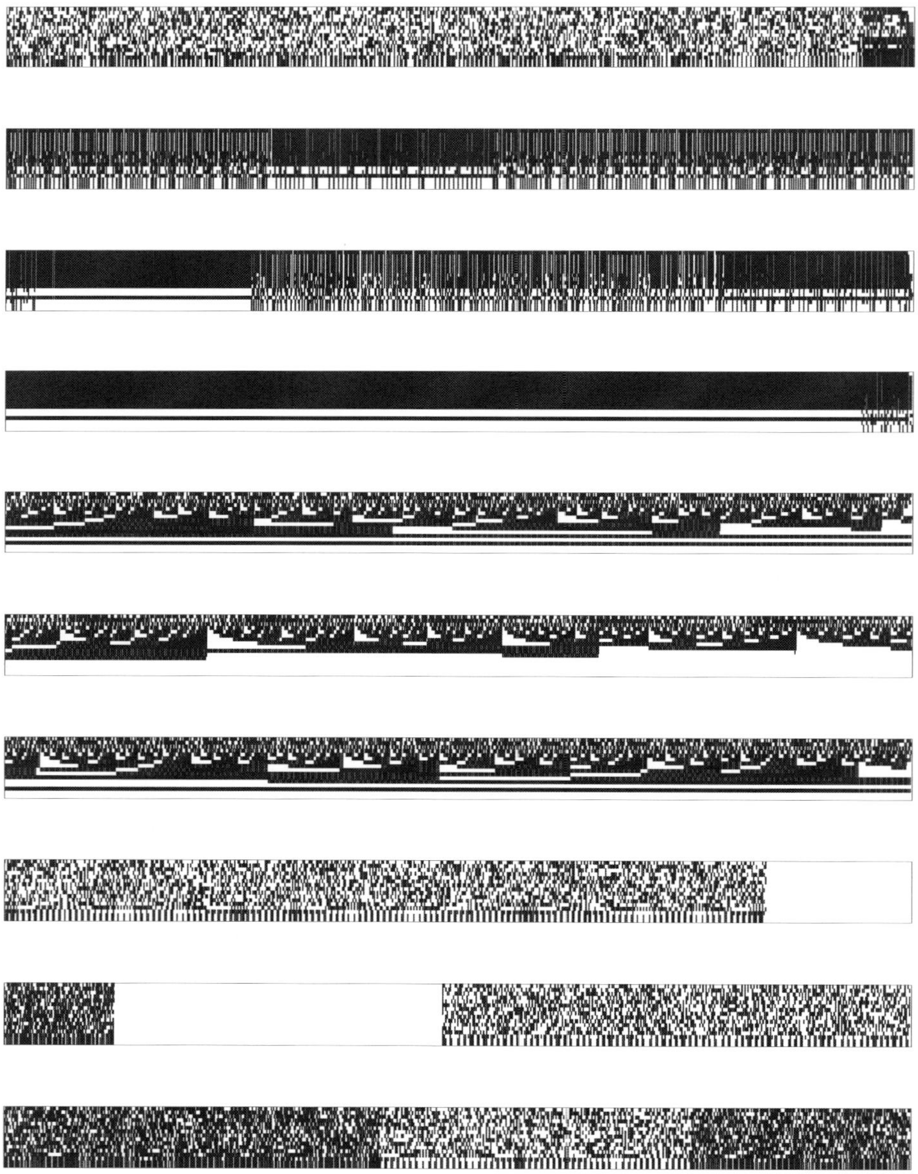

dataphonics 04 transformation 02:00 - 04:00 right

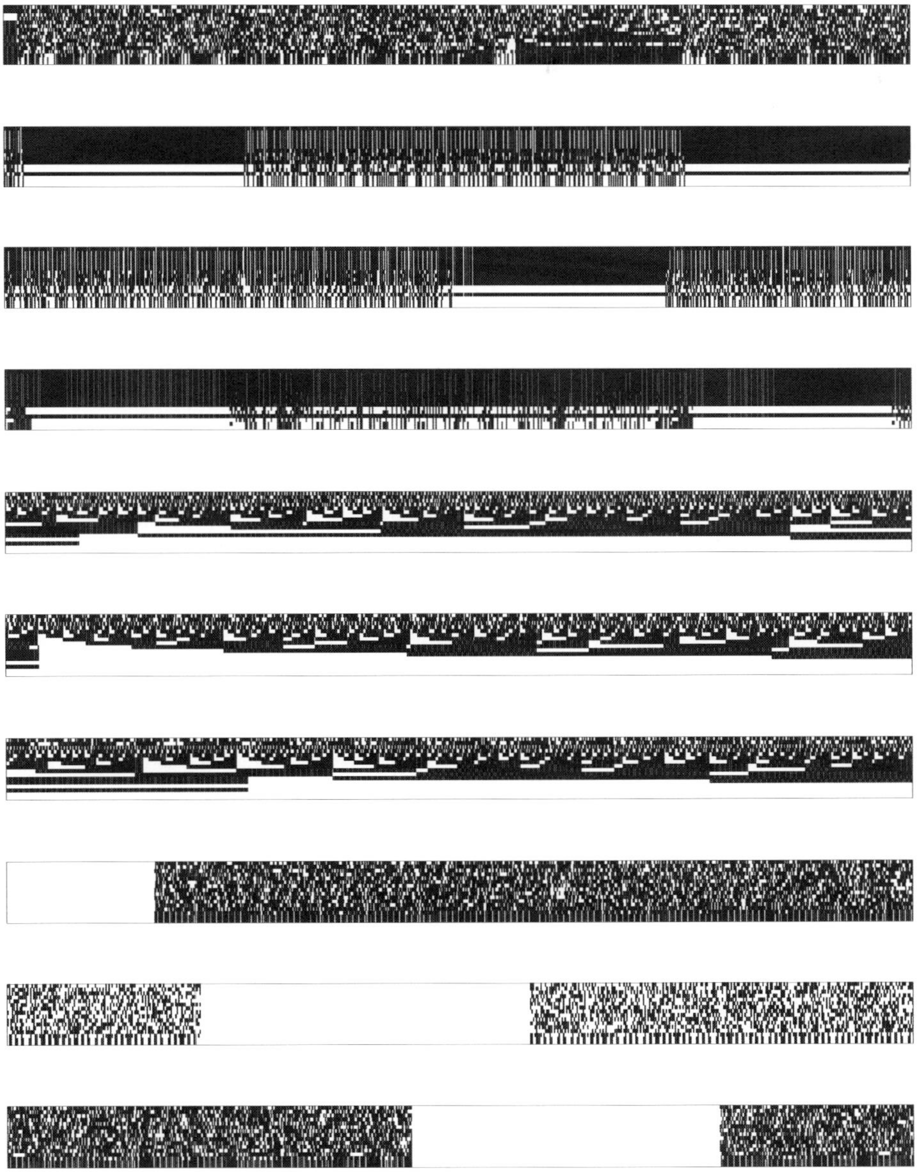

dataphonics 04 transformation 04:00 - 06:00 left

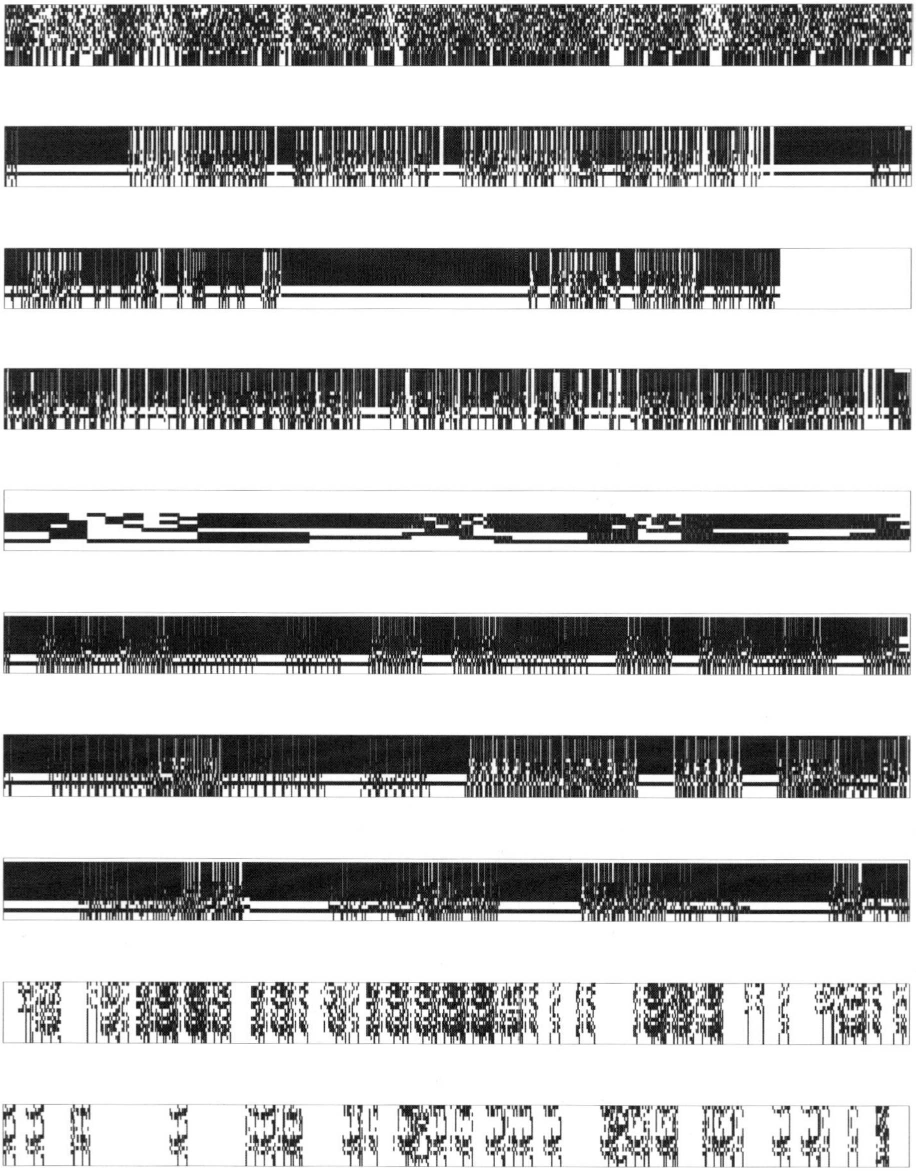

dataphonics 04 transformation 04:00 - 06:00 right

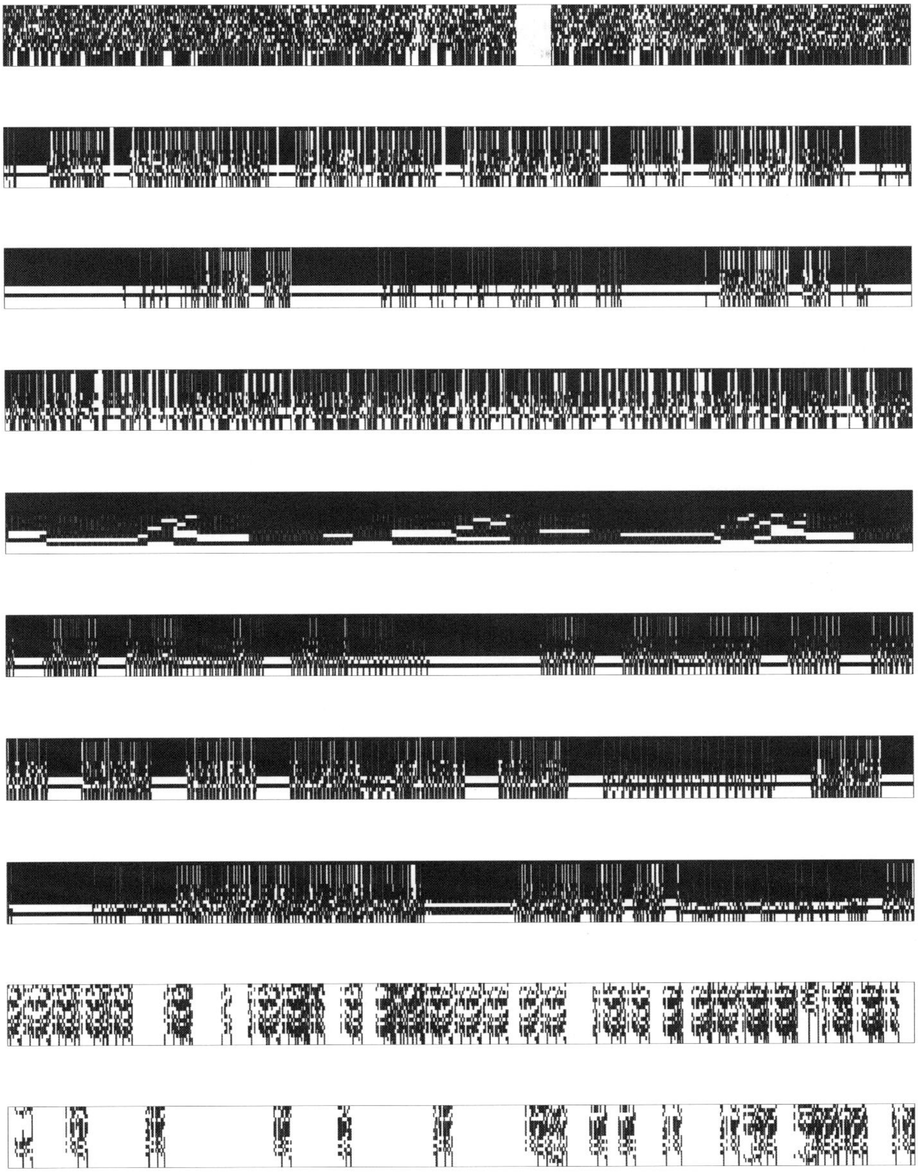

dataphonics 05 rhythmics 00:00 - 02:00 left

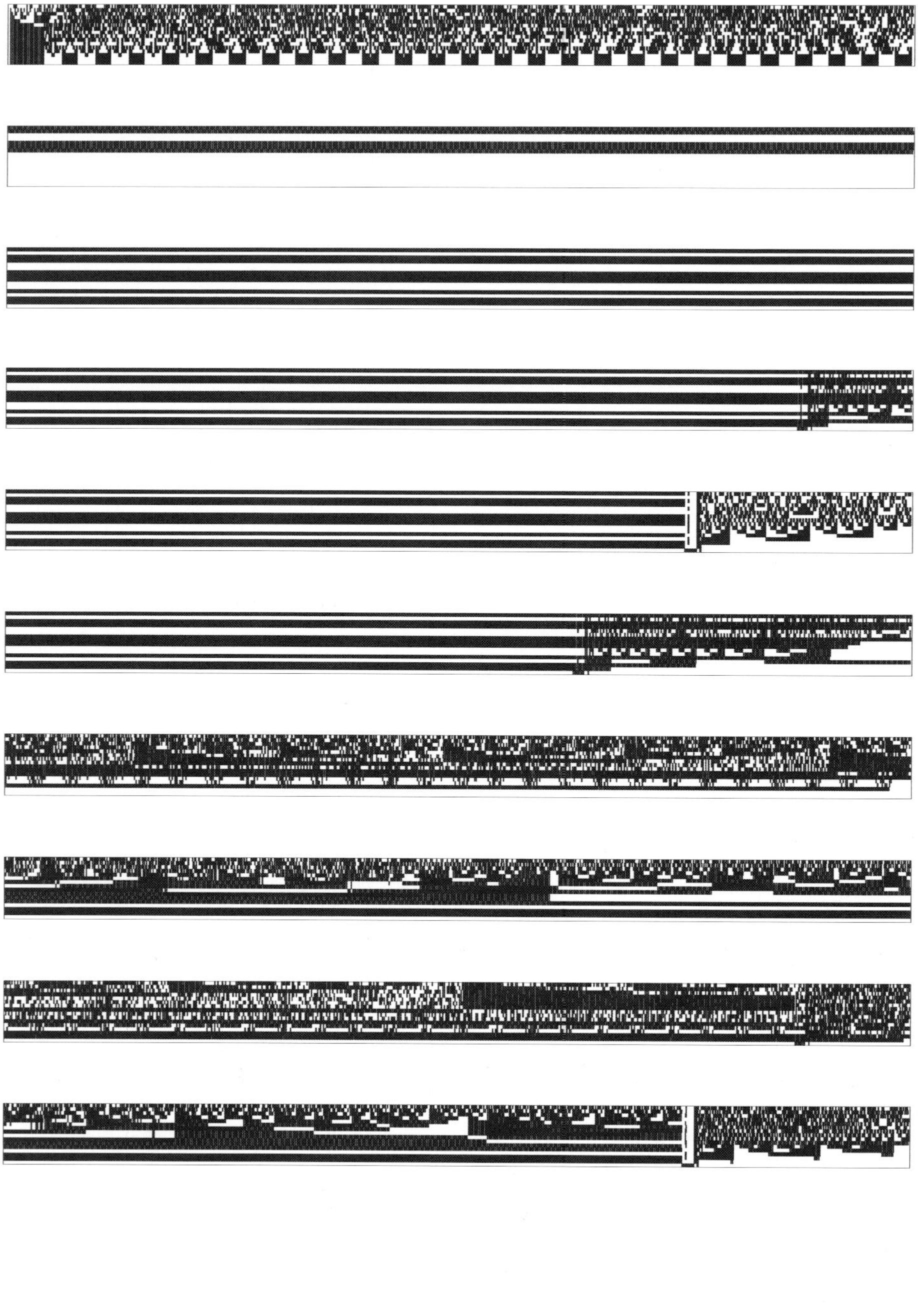

dataphonics 05 rhythmics 00:00 - 02:00 right

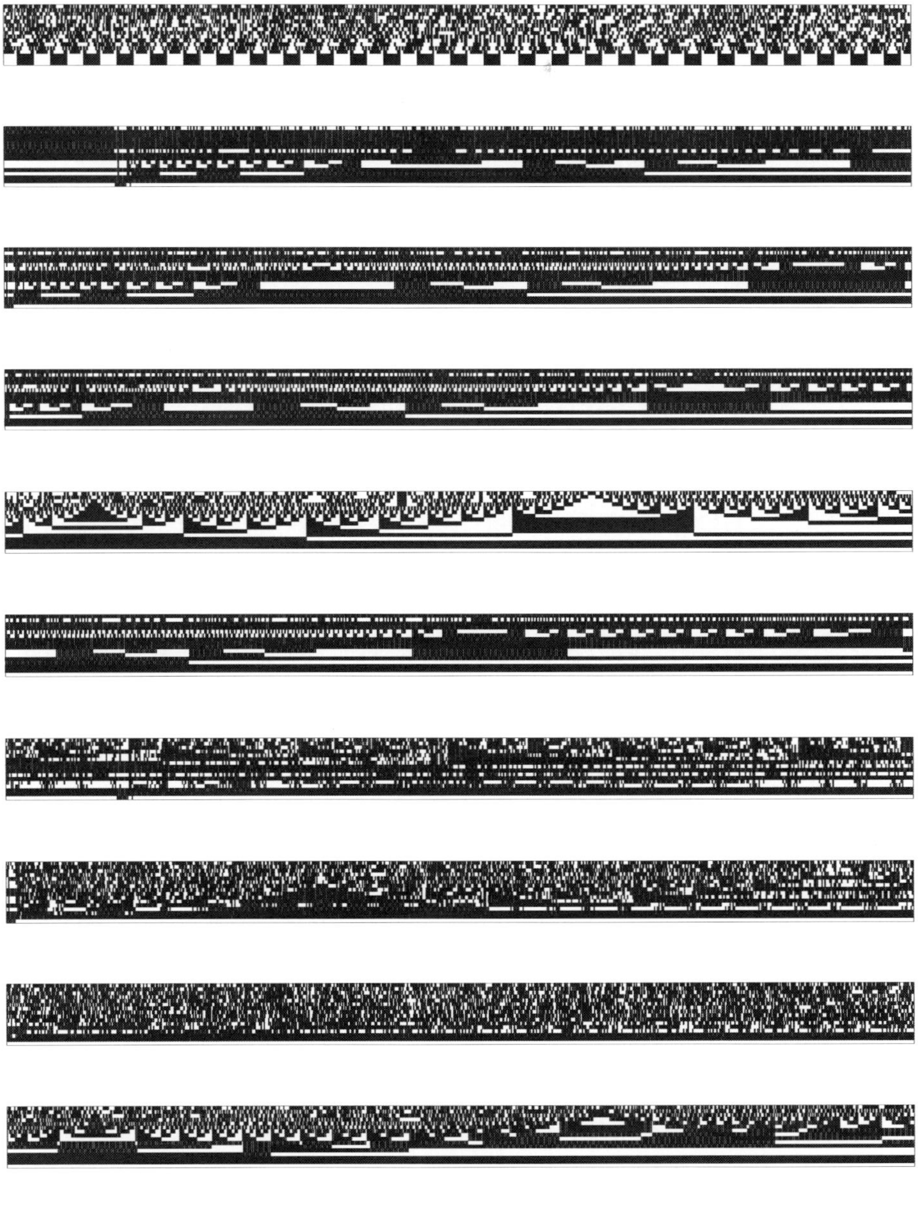

dataphonics 05 rhythmics 02:00 - 04:00 left

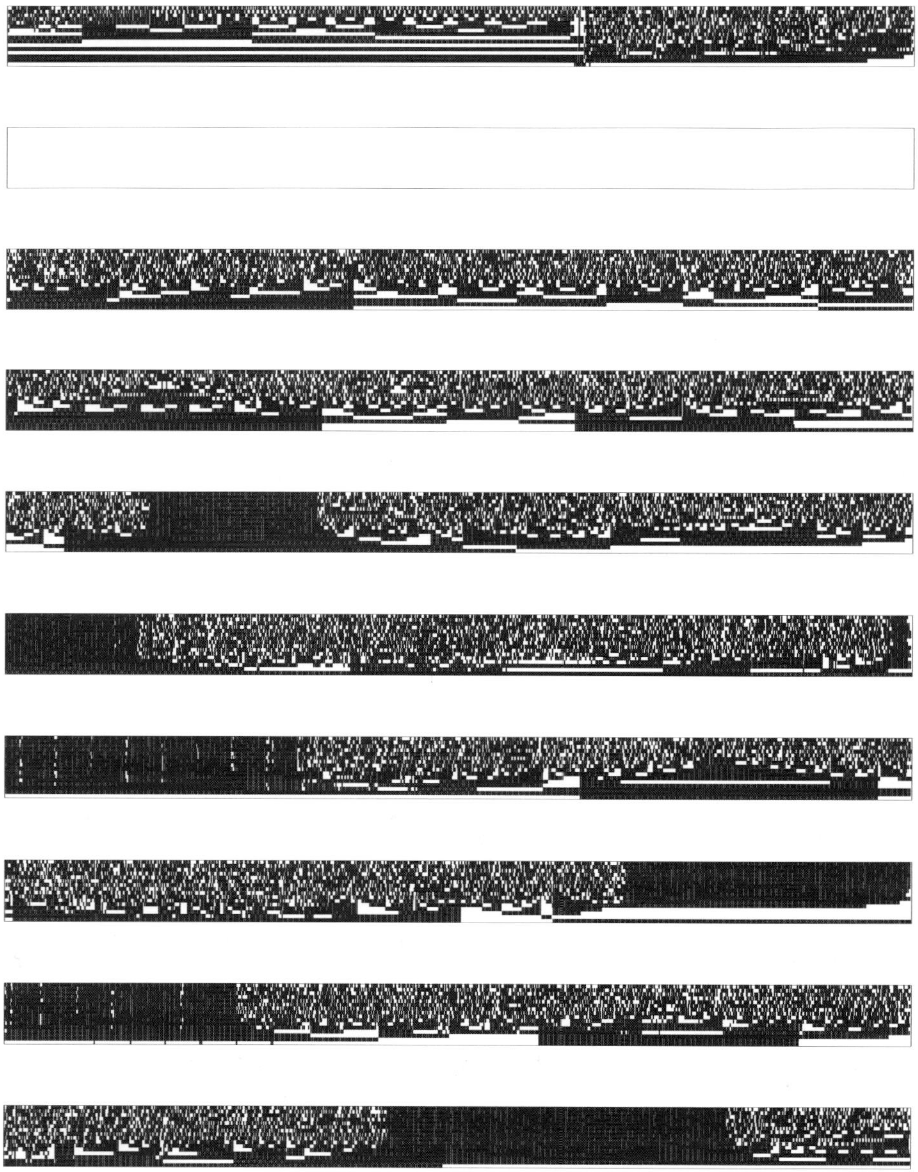

dataphonics 05 rhythmics 02:00 - 04:00 right

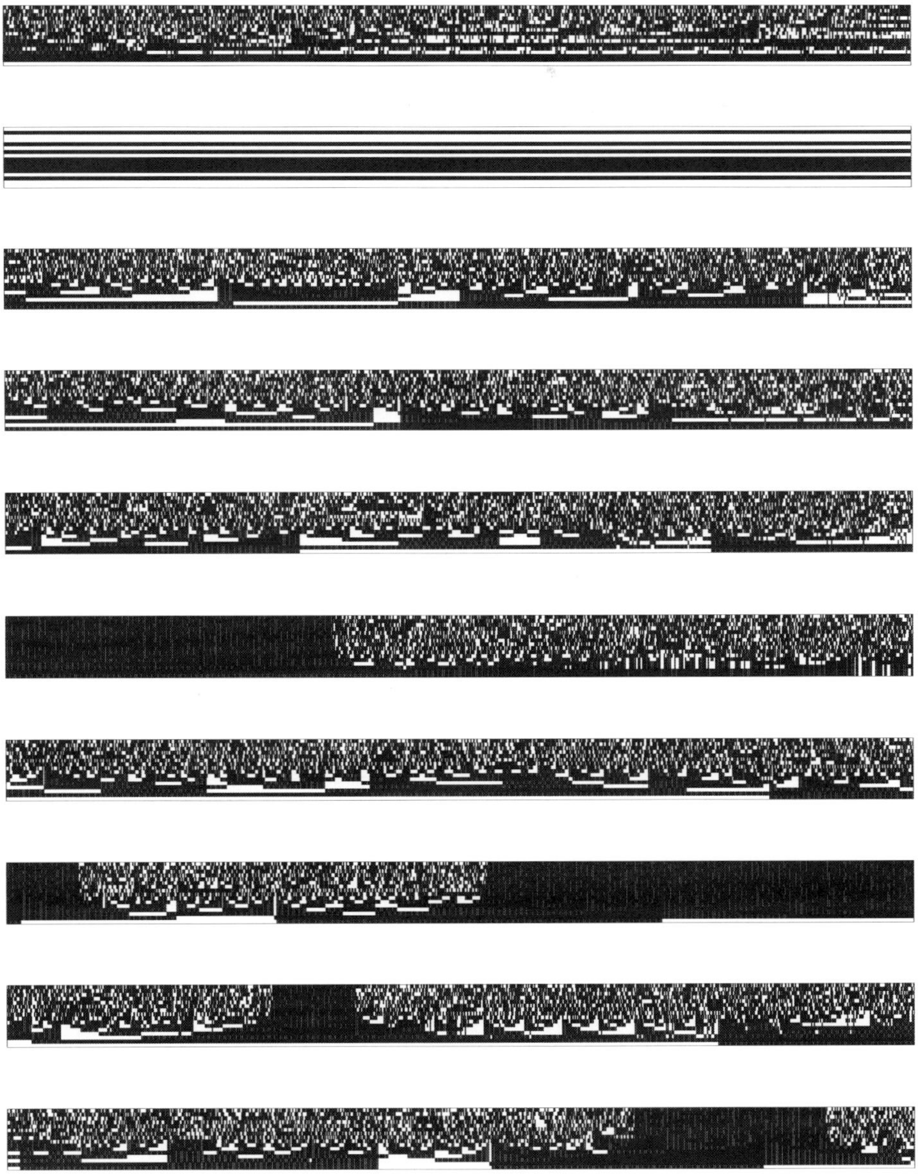

dataphonics 05 rhythmics 04:00 - 06:00 left

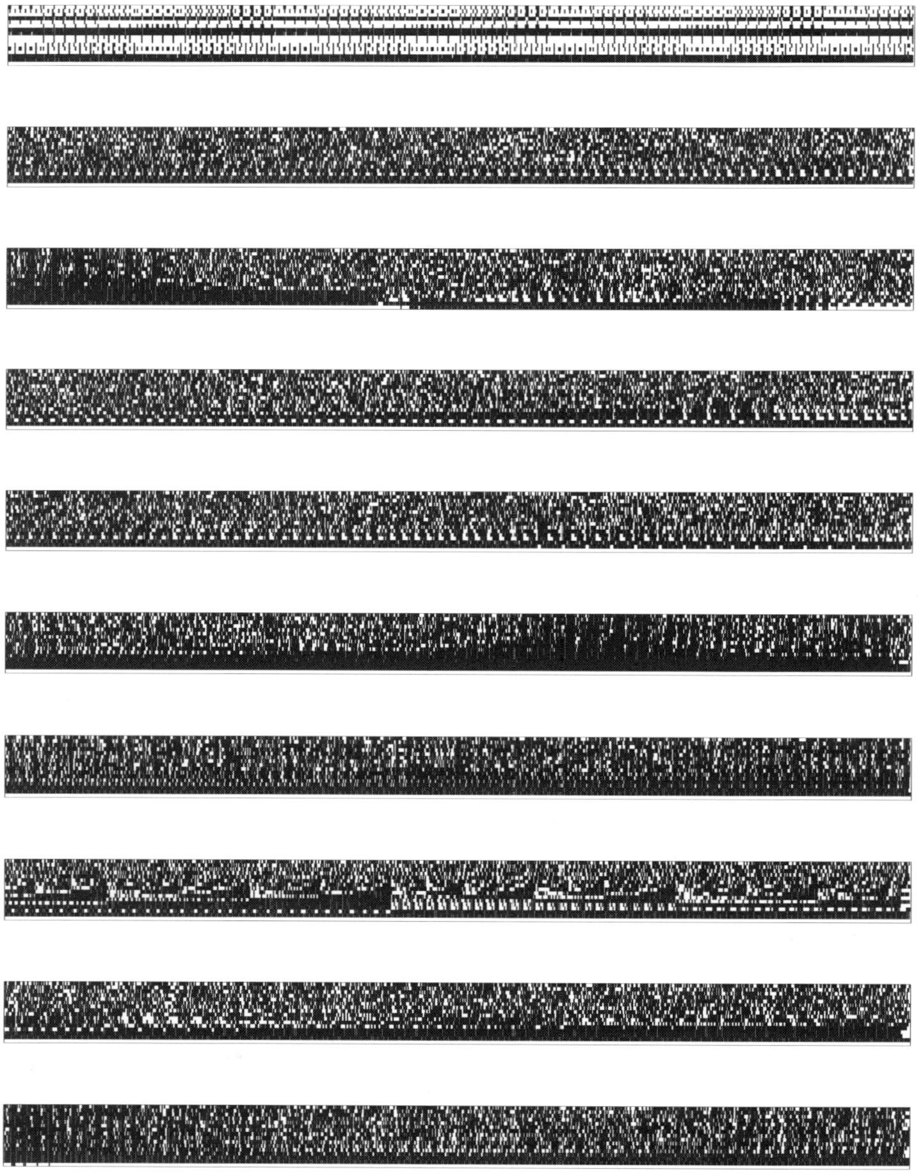

dataphonics 05 rhythmics 04:00 - 06:00 right

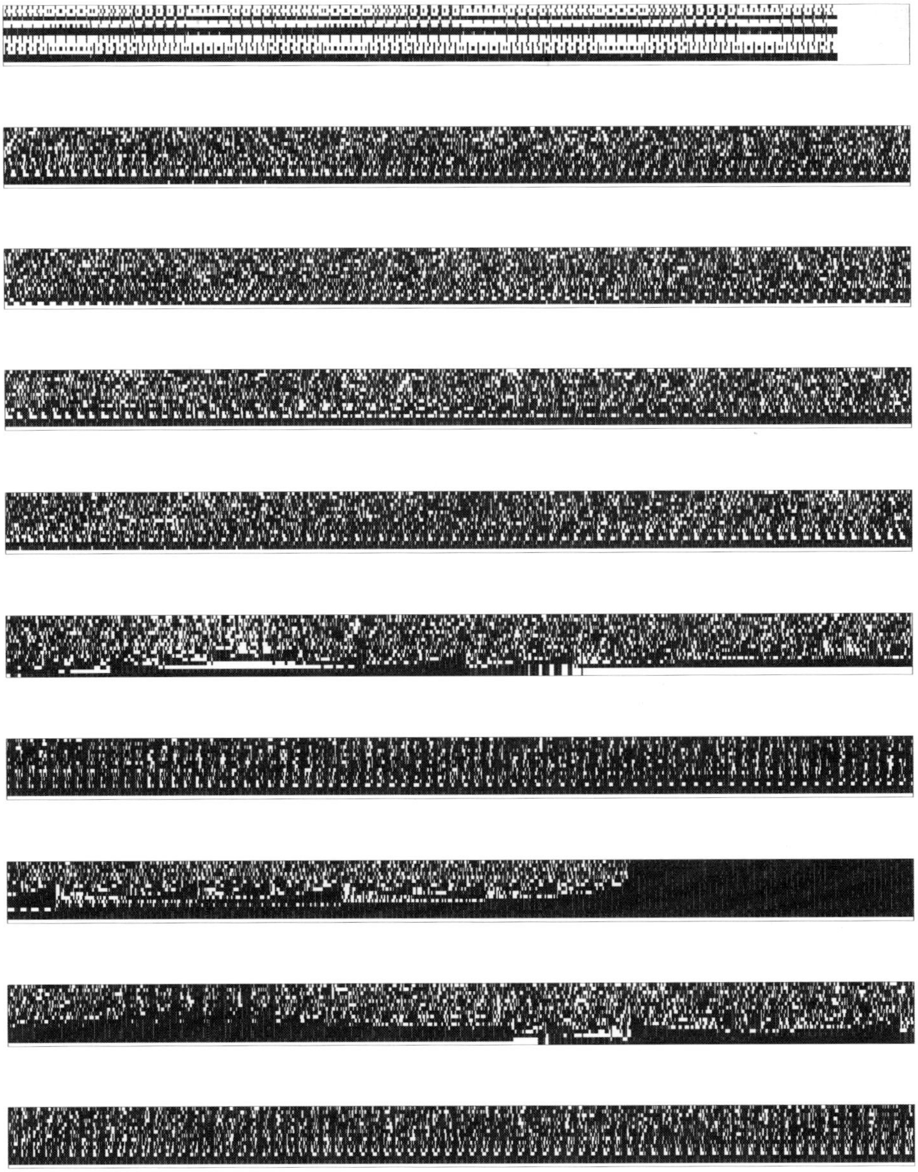

dataphonics 06 automatic 00:00 - 03:00 left

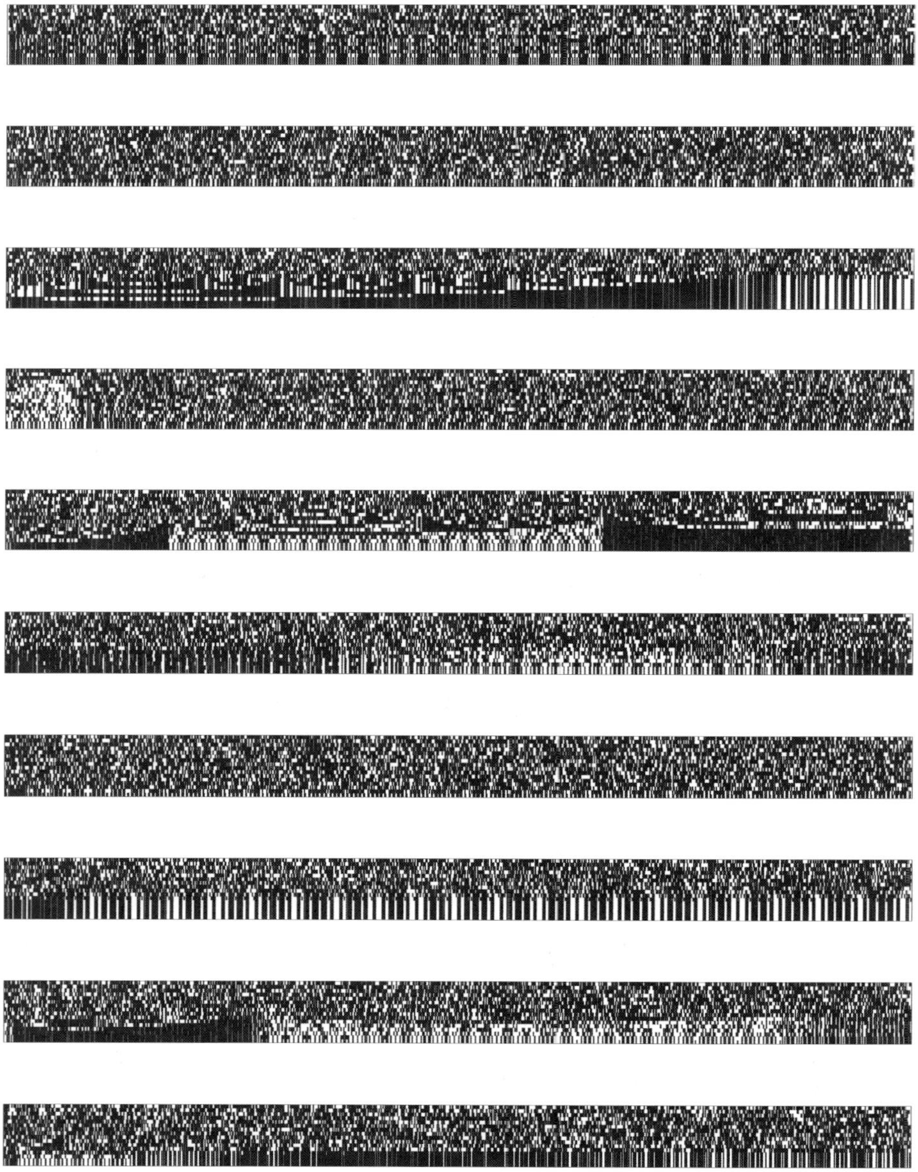

dataphonics 06 | automatic | 00:00 - 03:00 | right

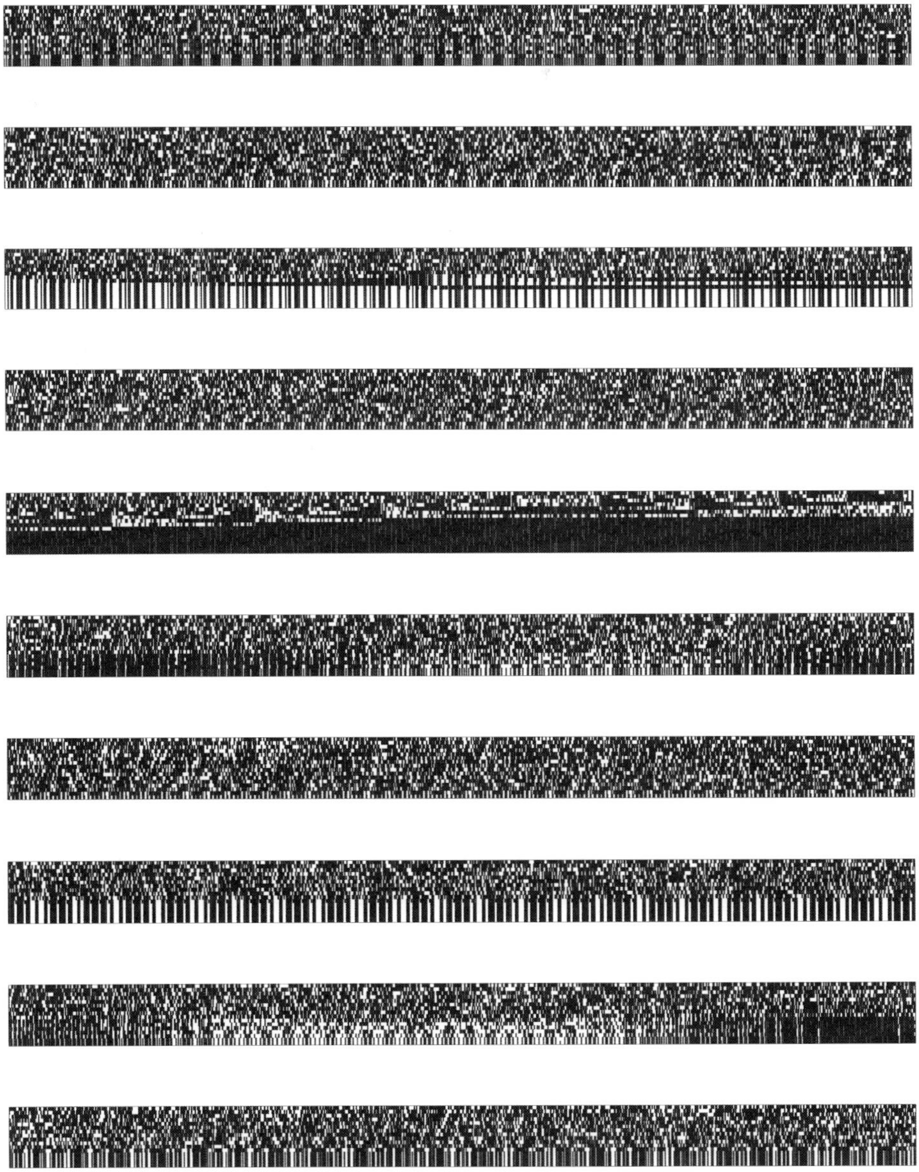

dataphonics 06 automatic 03:00 - 06:00 left

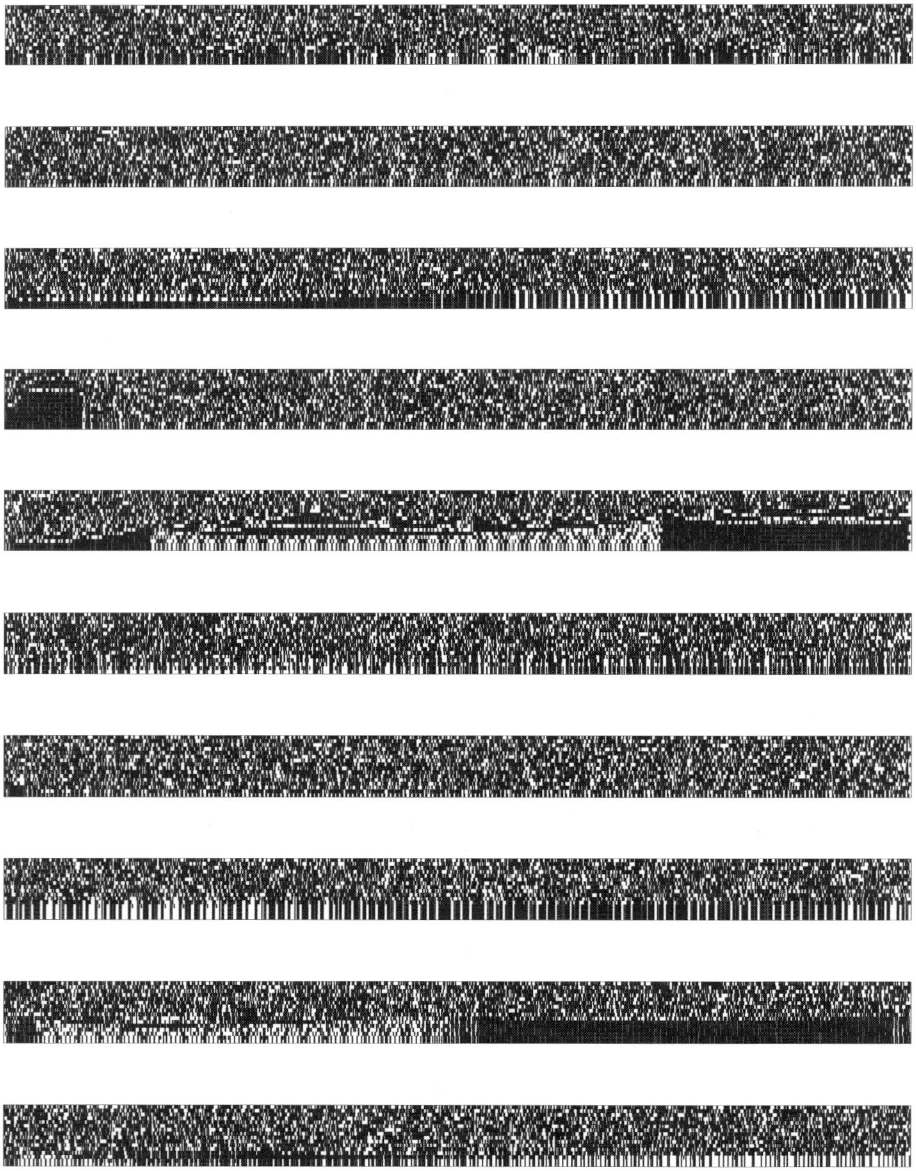

dataphonics 06 automatic 03:00 - 06:00 right

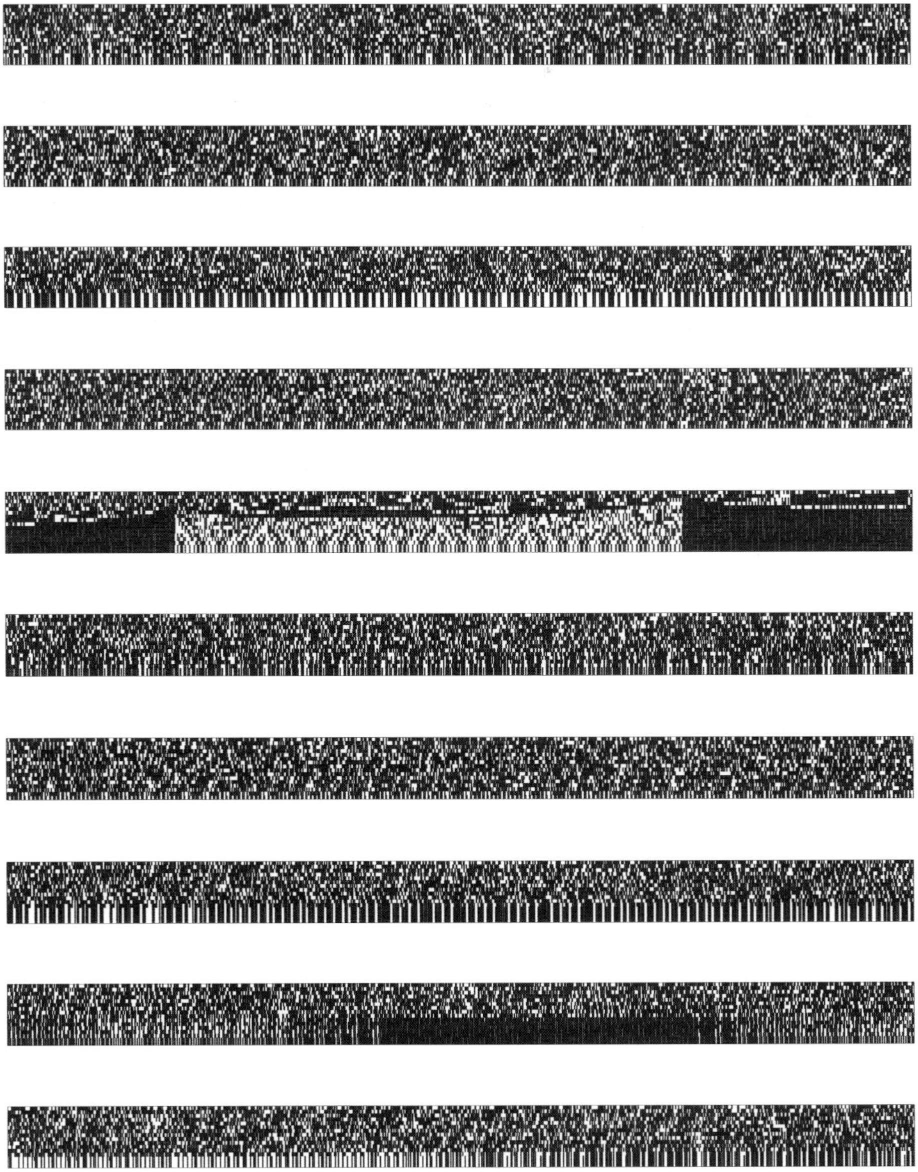

dataphonics 07 quantization 00:00 - 02:00 left

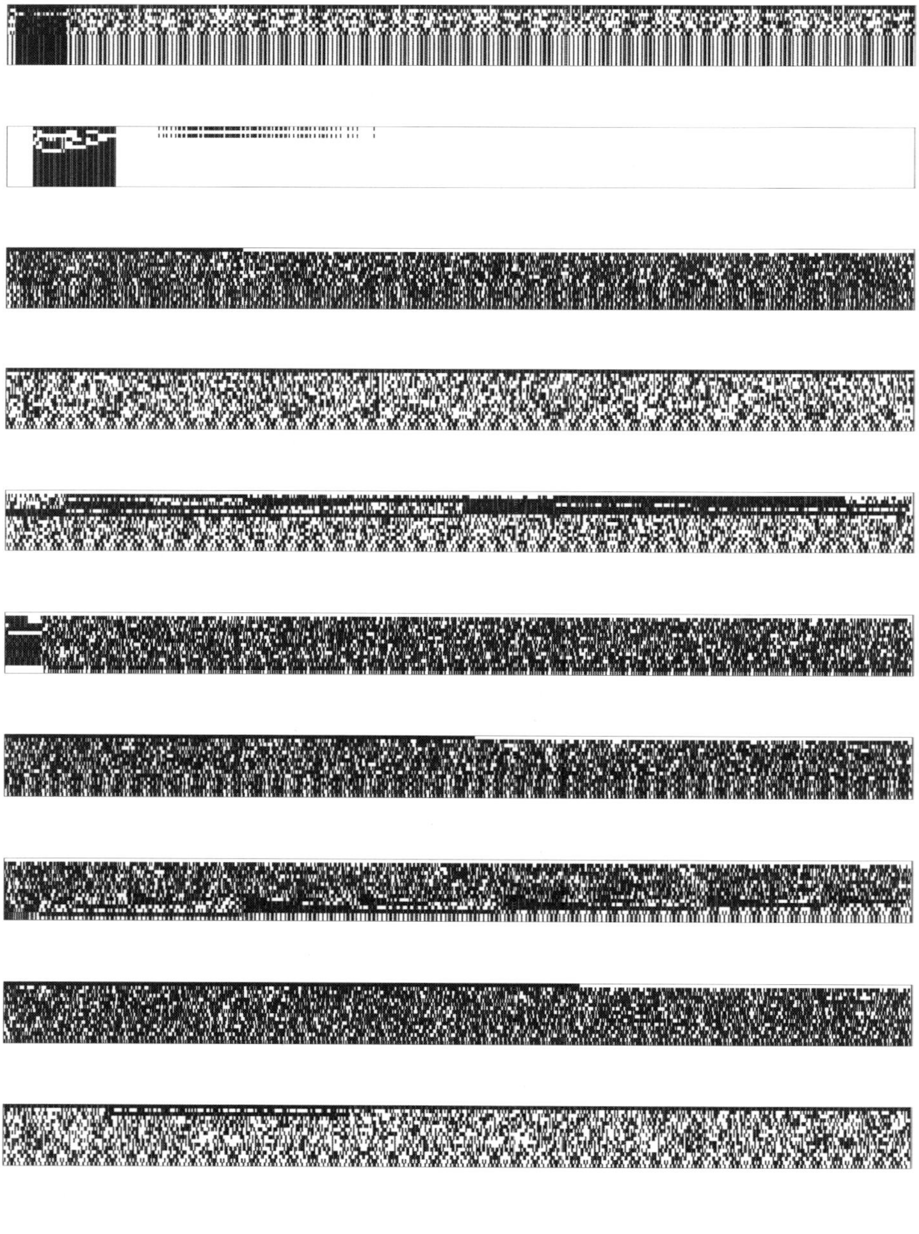

dataphonics 07 quantization 00:00 - 02:00 right

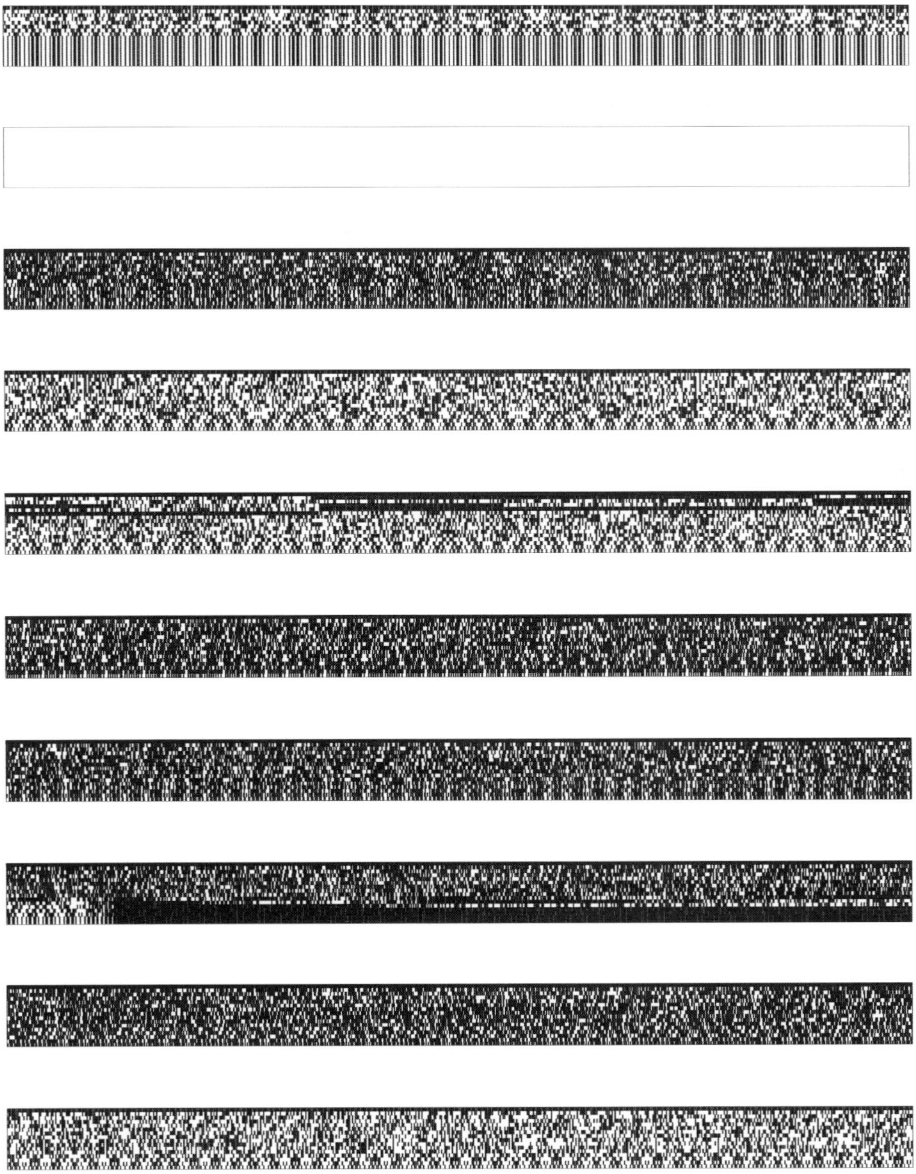

dataphonics 07 quantization 02:00 - 04:00 left

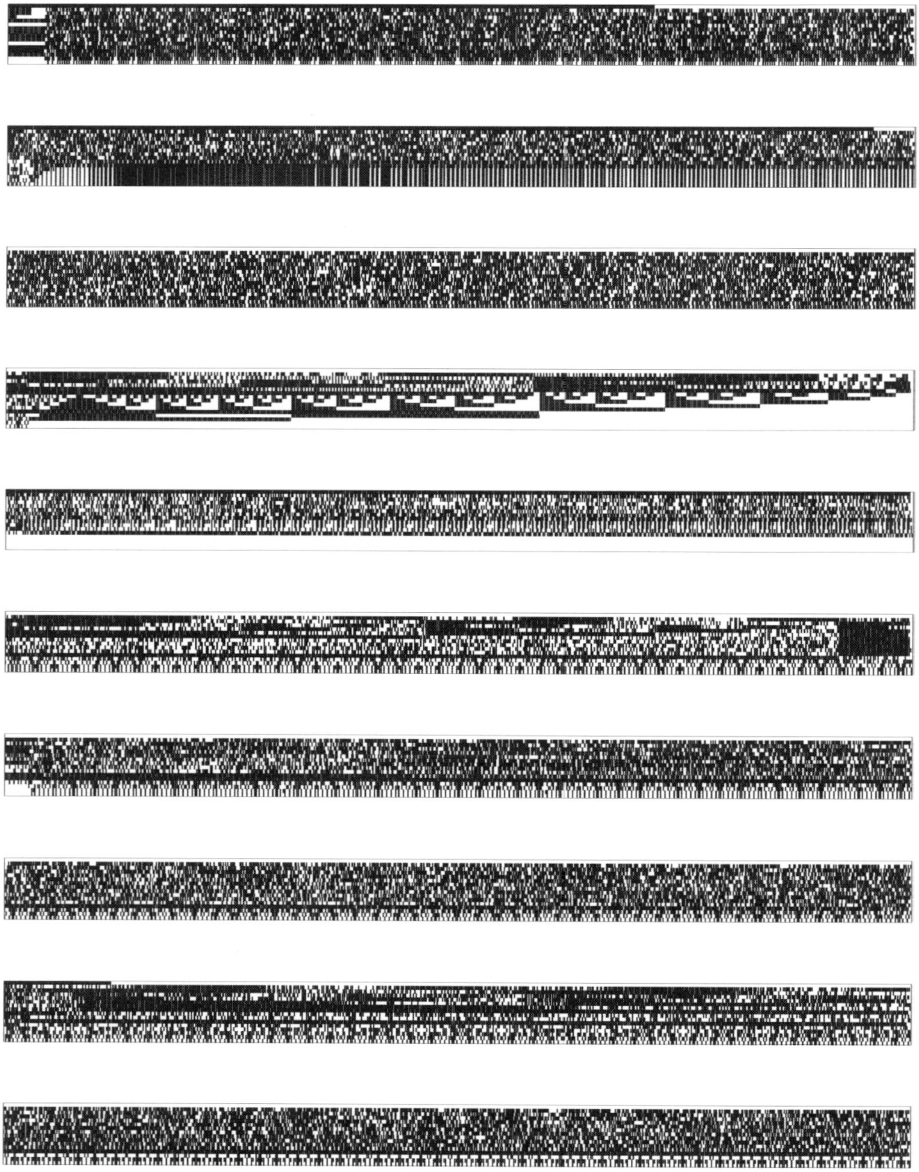

dataphonics 07 quantization 02:00 - 04:00 right

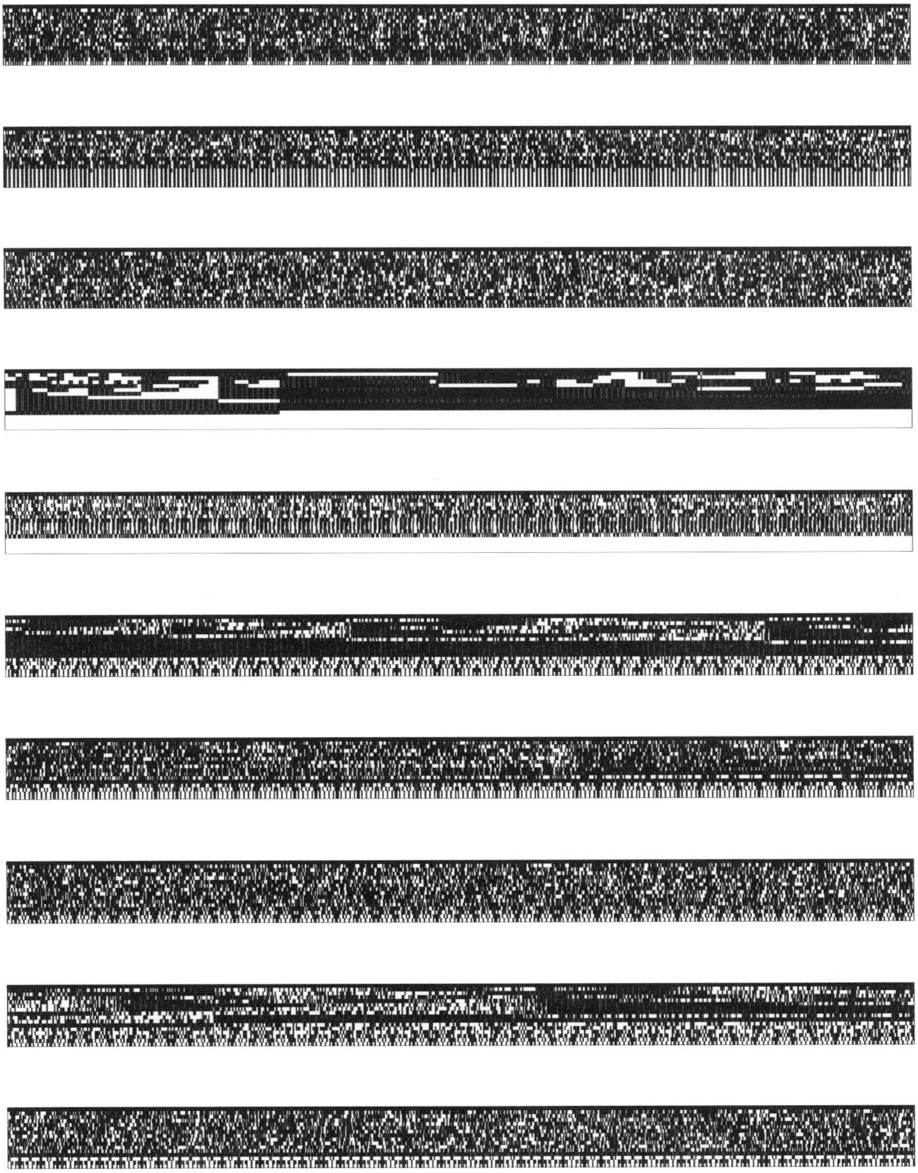

dataphonics 07 quantization 04:00 - 06:00 left

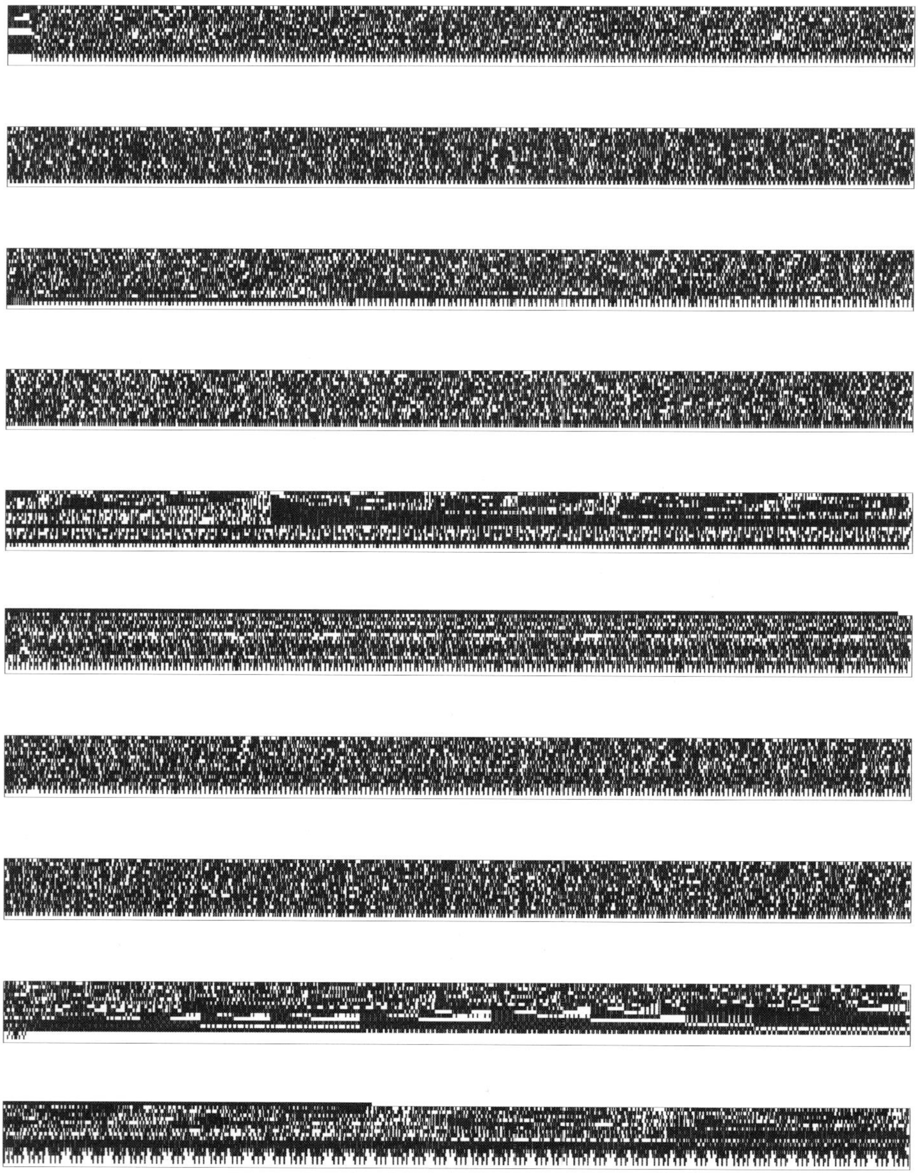

dataphonics 07 quantization 04:00 - 06:00 right

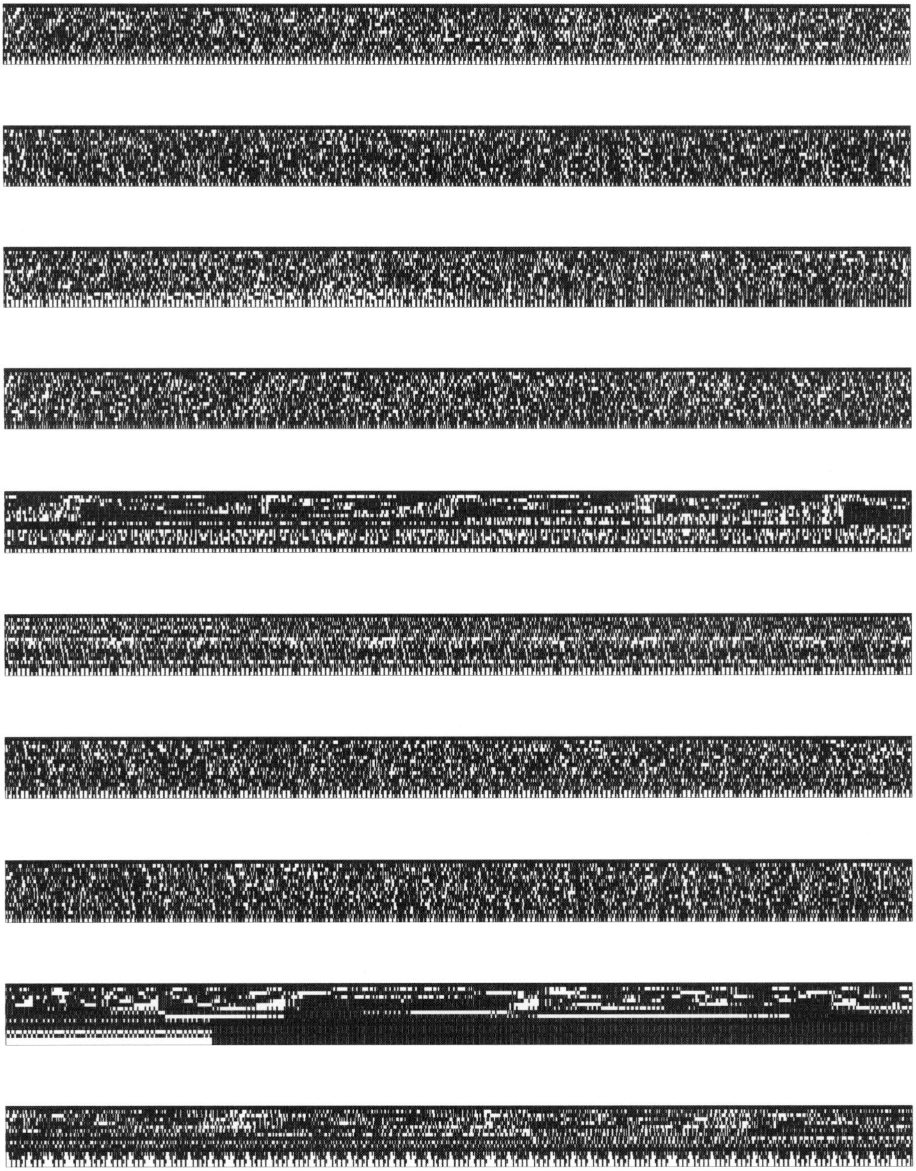

dataphonics 08 harmonics 00:00 - 02:00 left

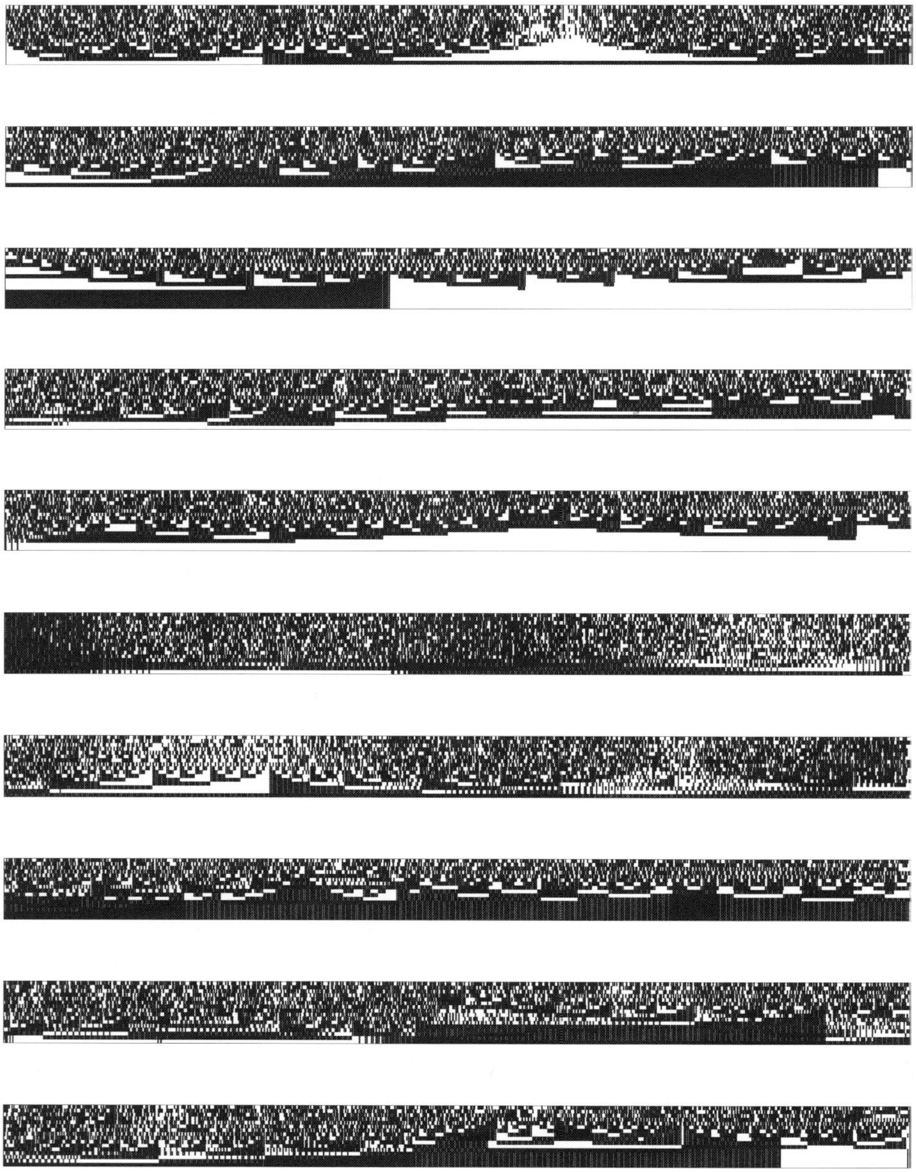

dataphonics 08 harmonics 00:00 - 02:00 right

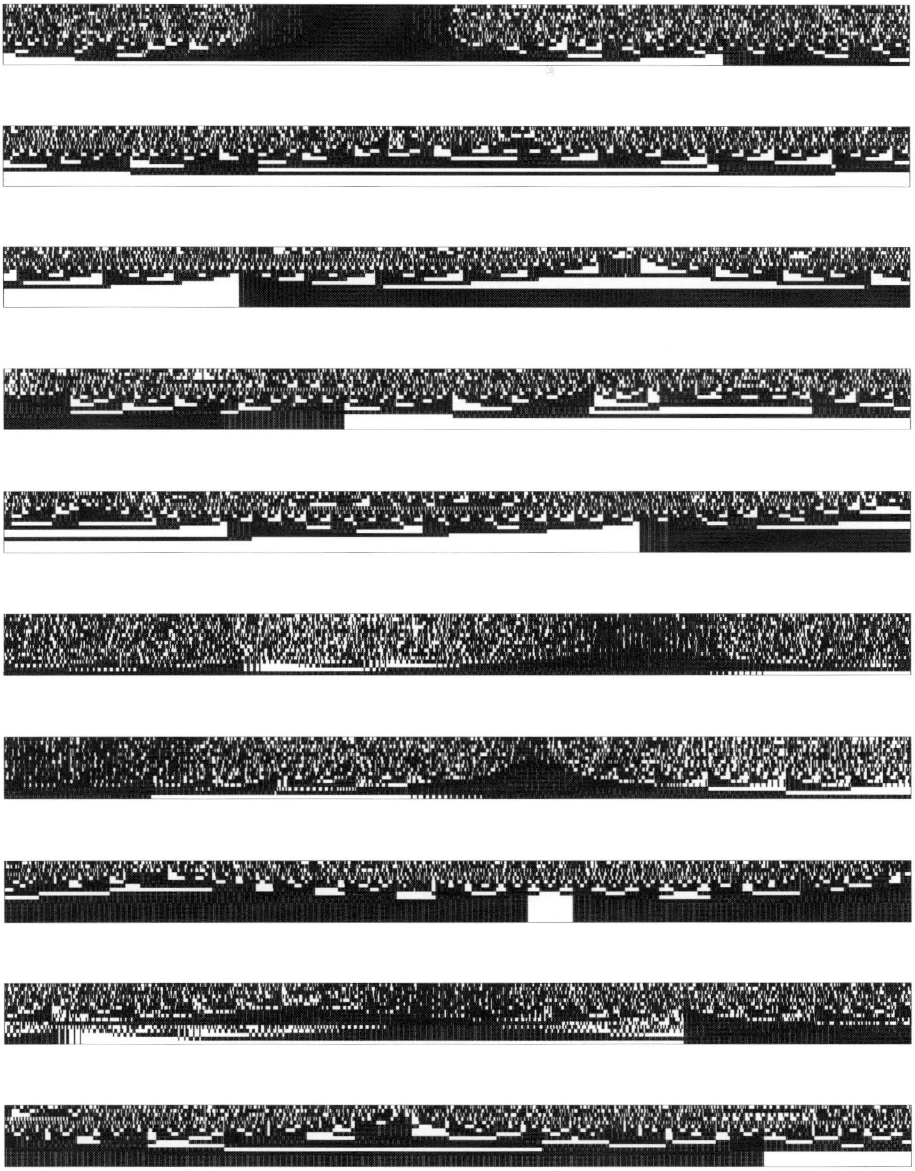

dataphonics 08 harmonics 02:00 - 04 00 left

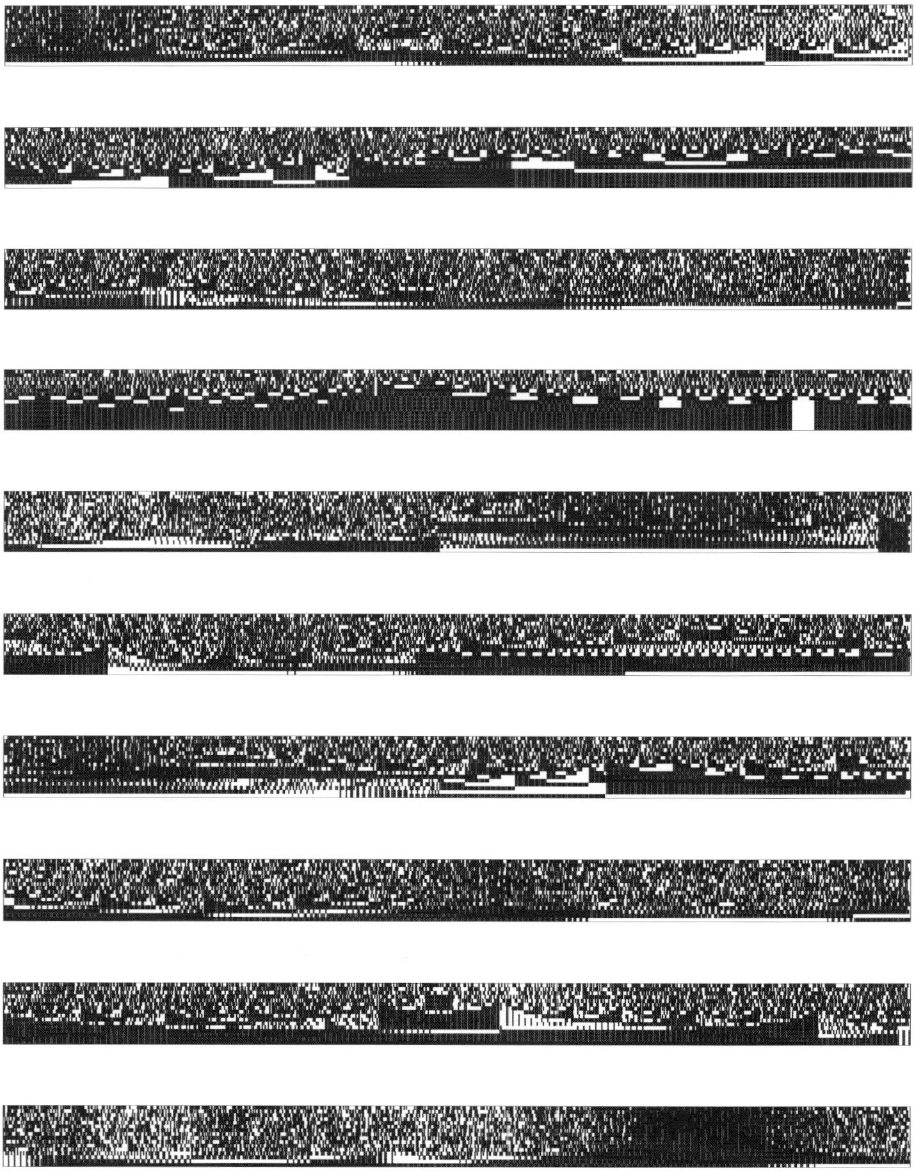

dataphonics 08 harmonics 02:00 - 04:00 right

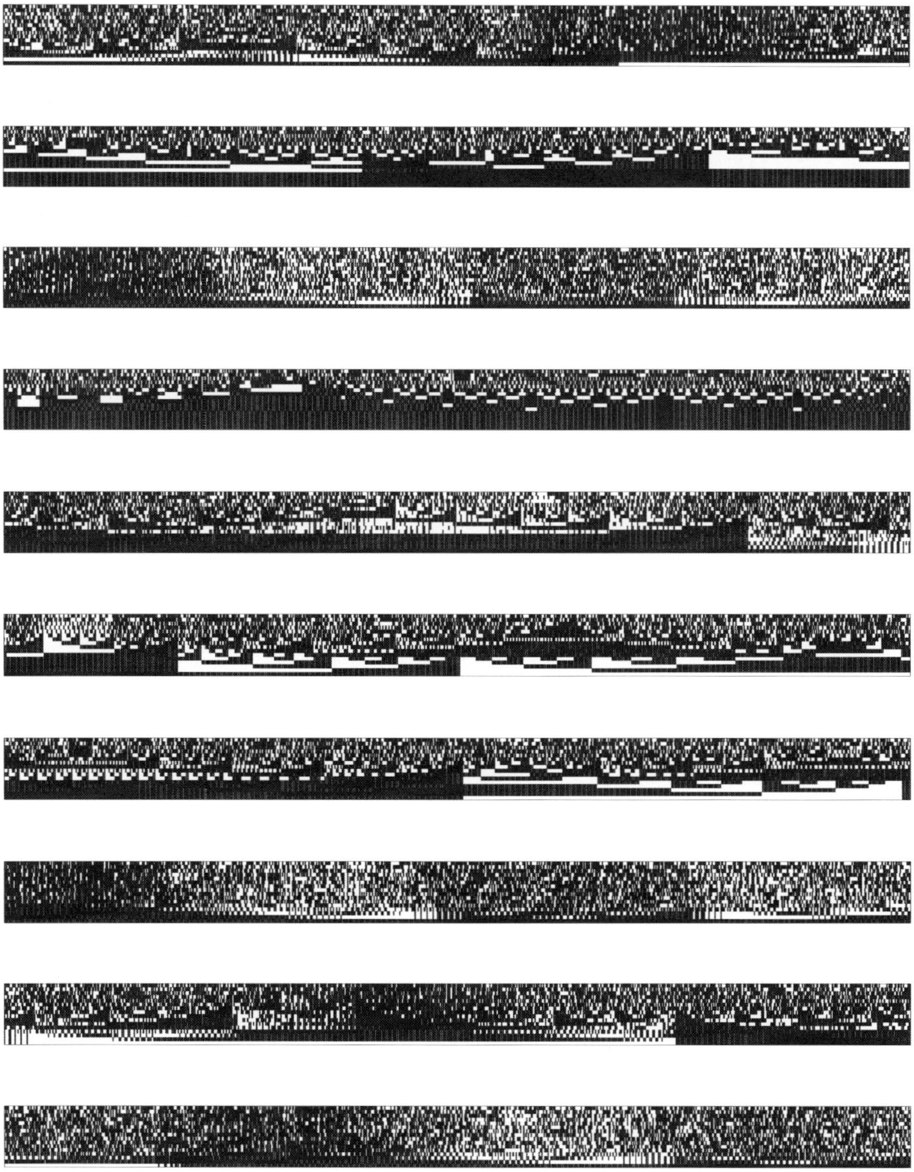

dataphonics 08 | harmonics | 04:00 - 06:00 | left

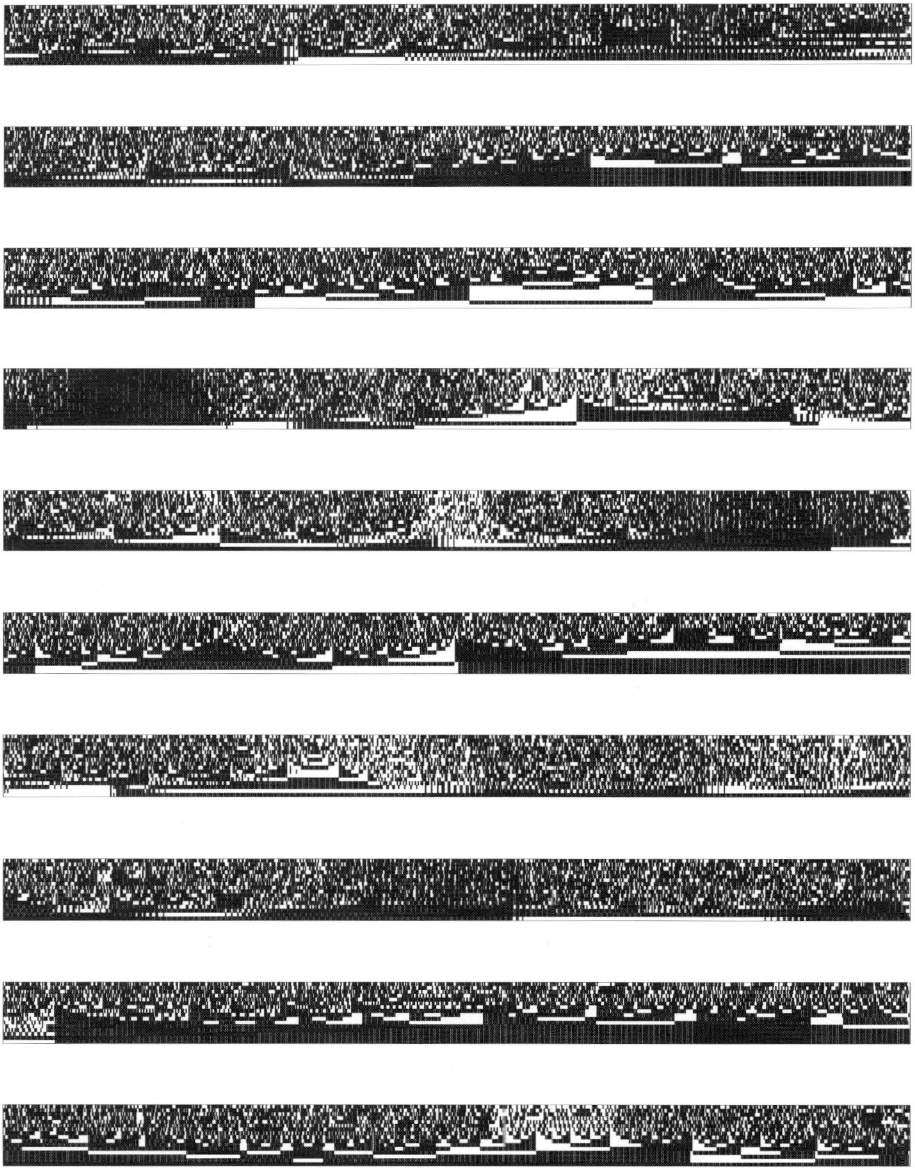

dataphonics 08 harmonics 04:00 - 06:00 right

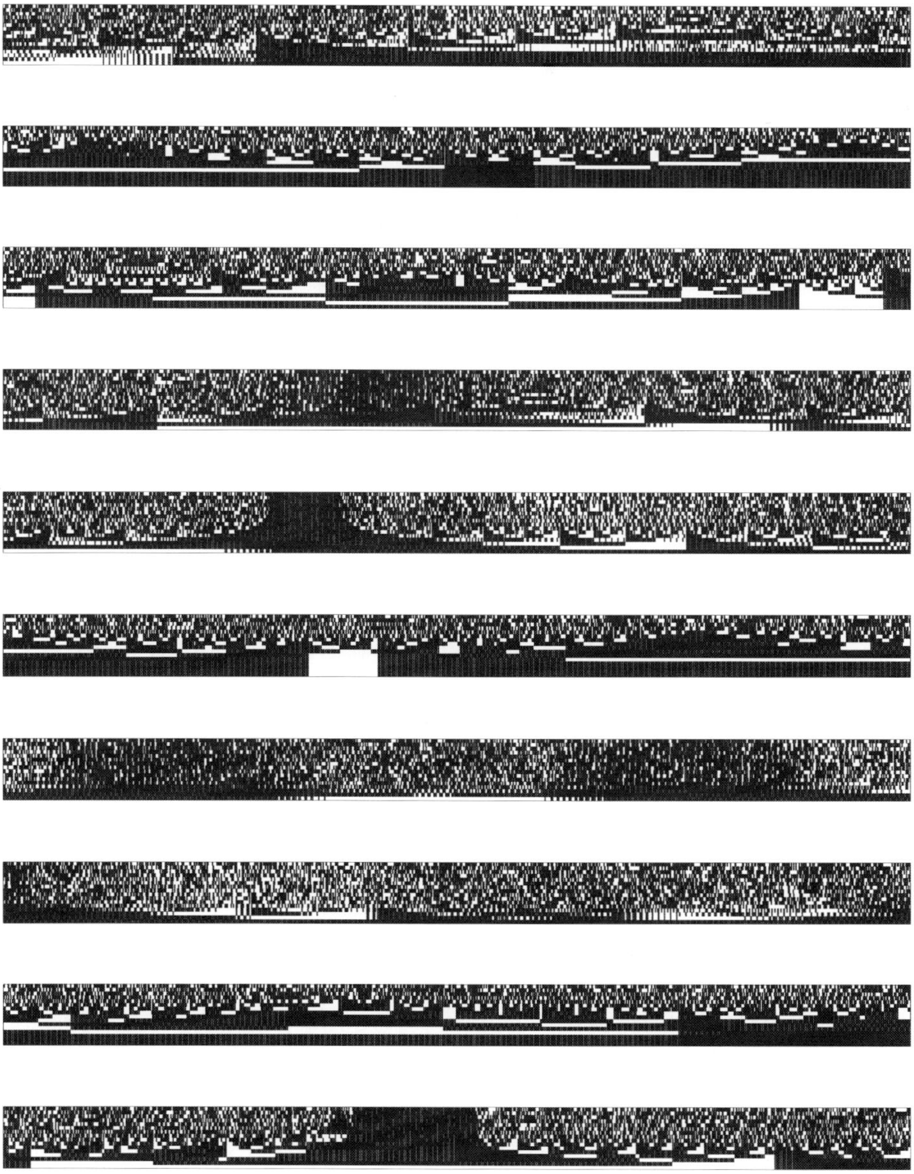

dataphonics 09 counterpoint 00:00 - 02:00 left

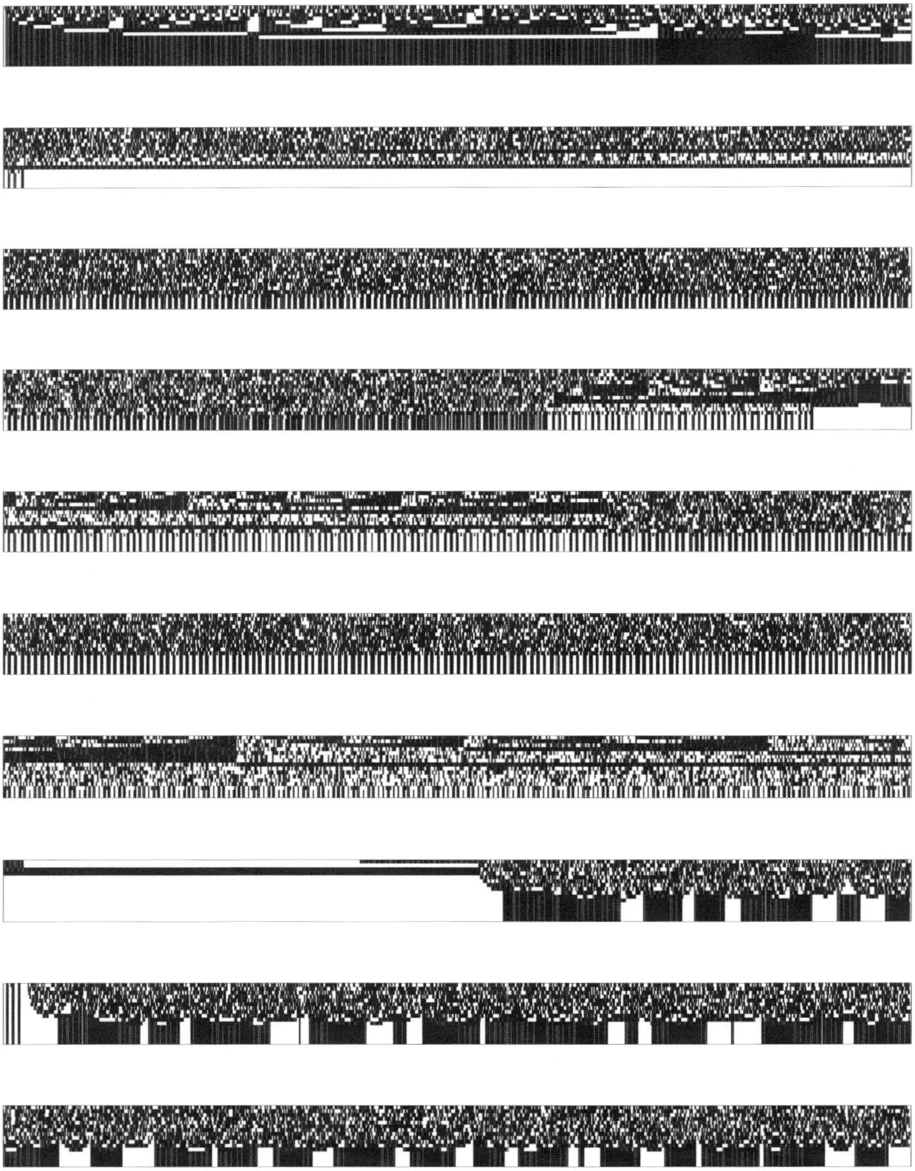

dataphonics 09 counterpoint 00:00 - 02:00 right

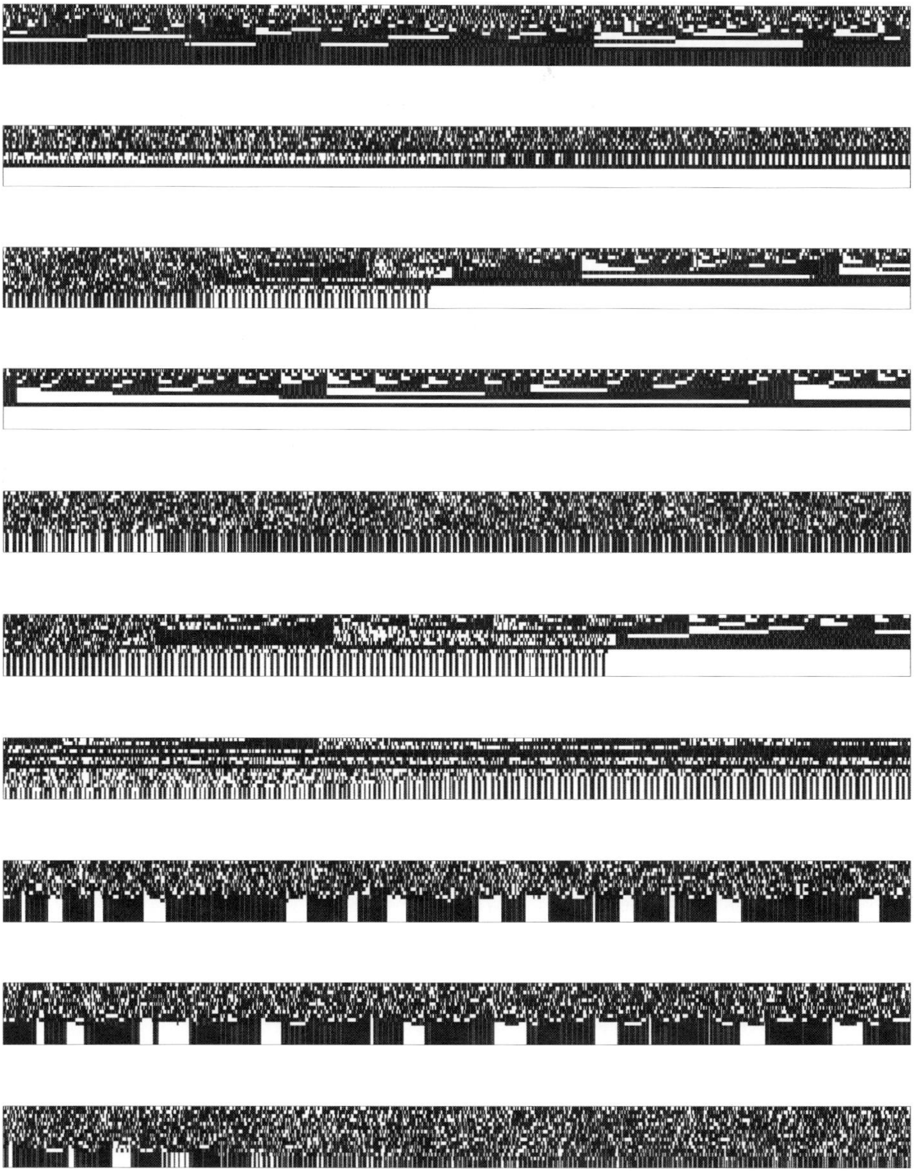

dataphonics 09 counterpoint 02:00 - 04:00 left

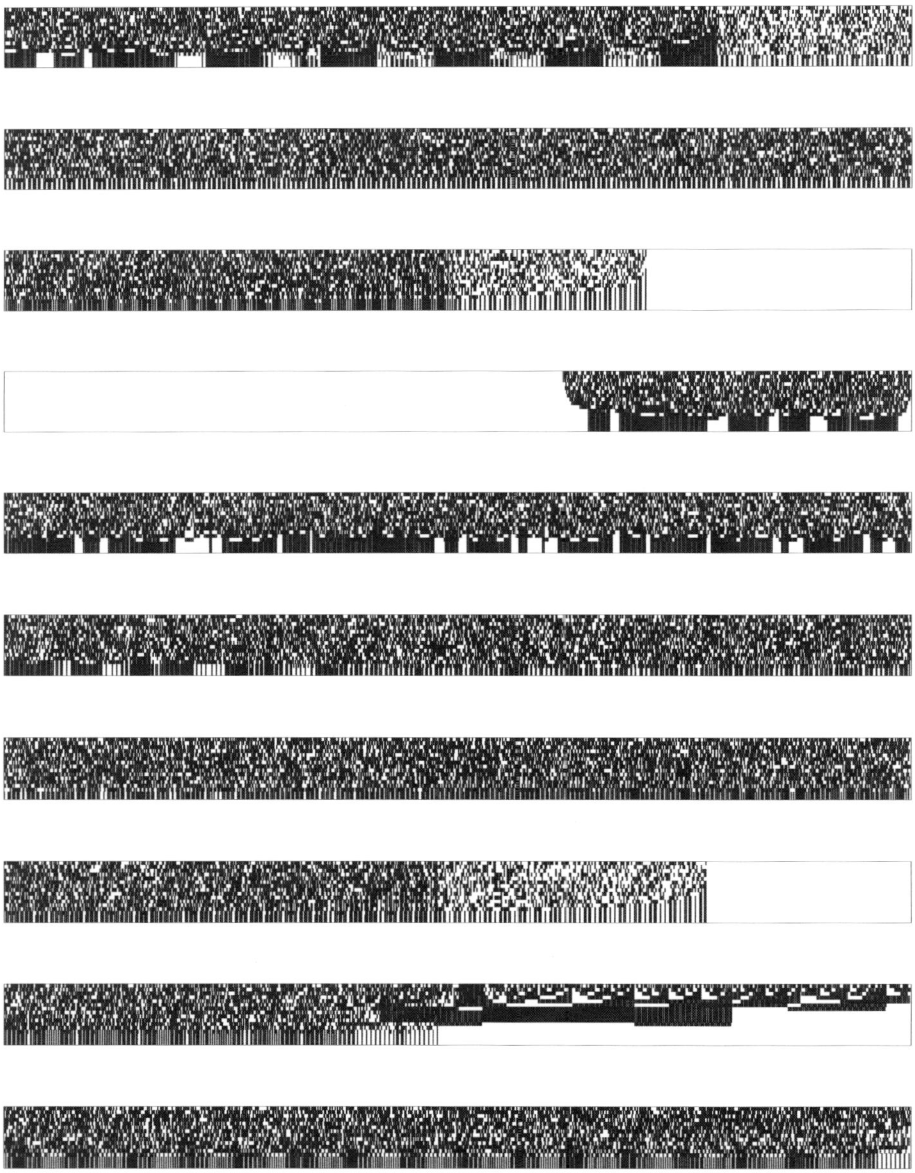

dataphonics 09 counterpoint 02:00 - 04:00 right

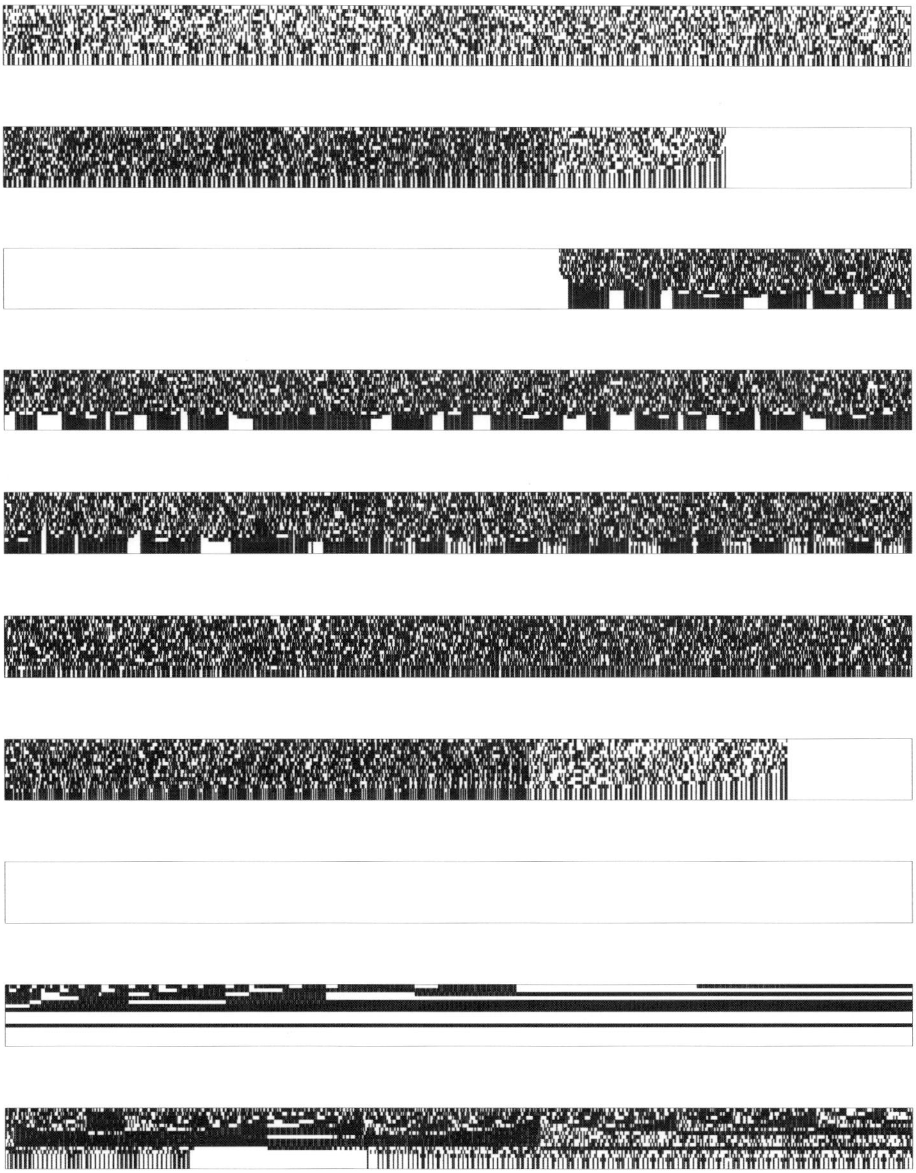

dataphonics 09 counterpoint 04:00 - 06:00 left

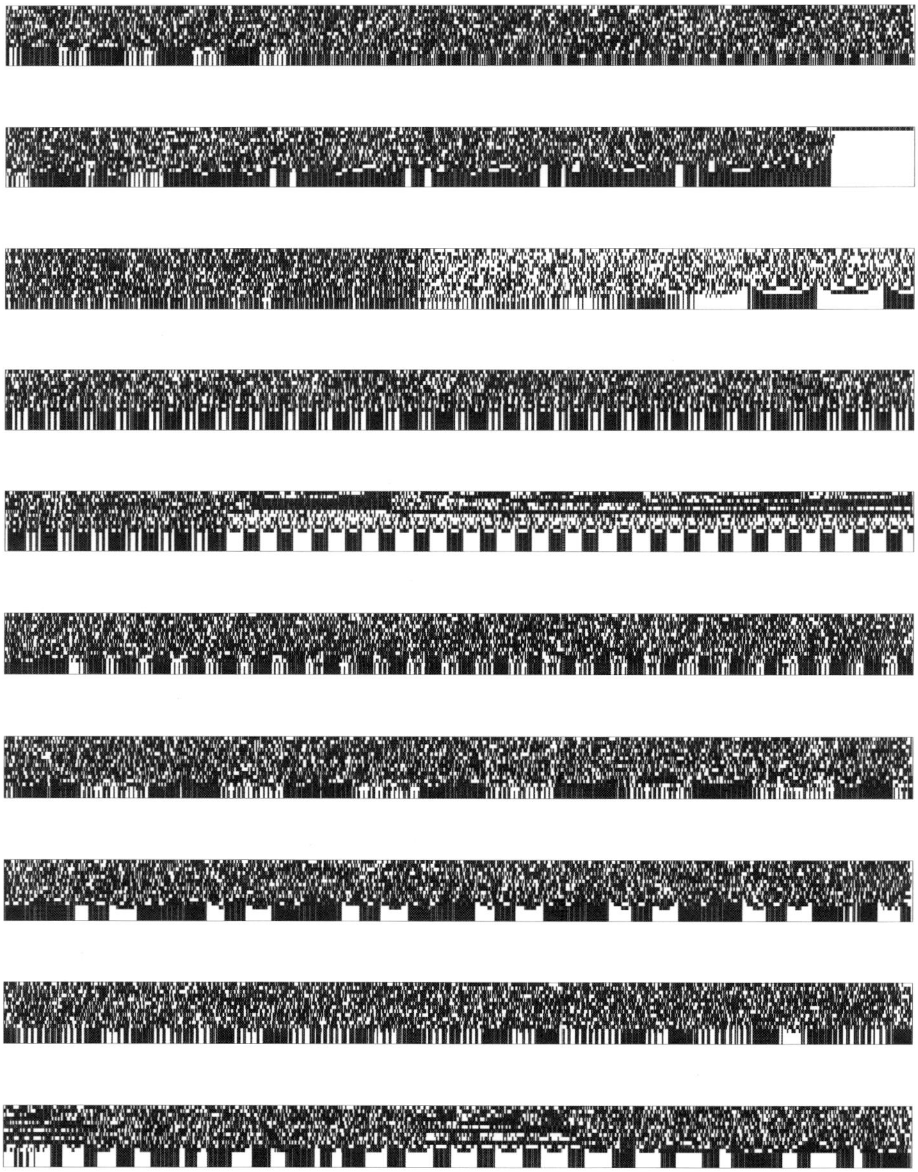

dataphonics 09 counterpoint 04:00 - 06:00 right

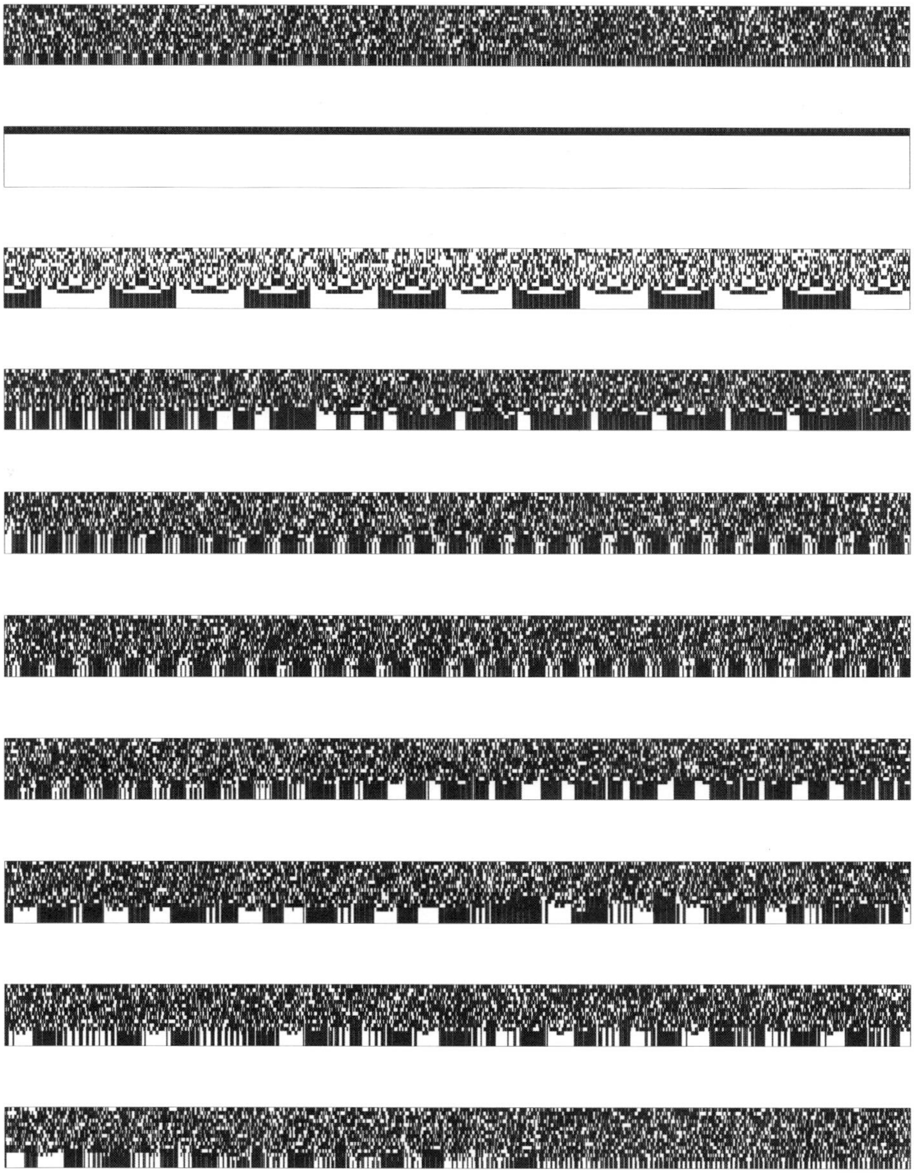

dataphonics 10 structure 00:00 - 03:00 left

dataphonics 10 structure 00:00 - 03:00 right

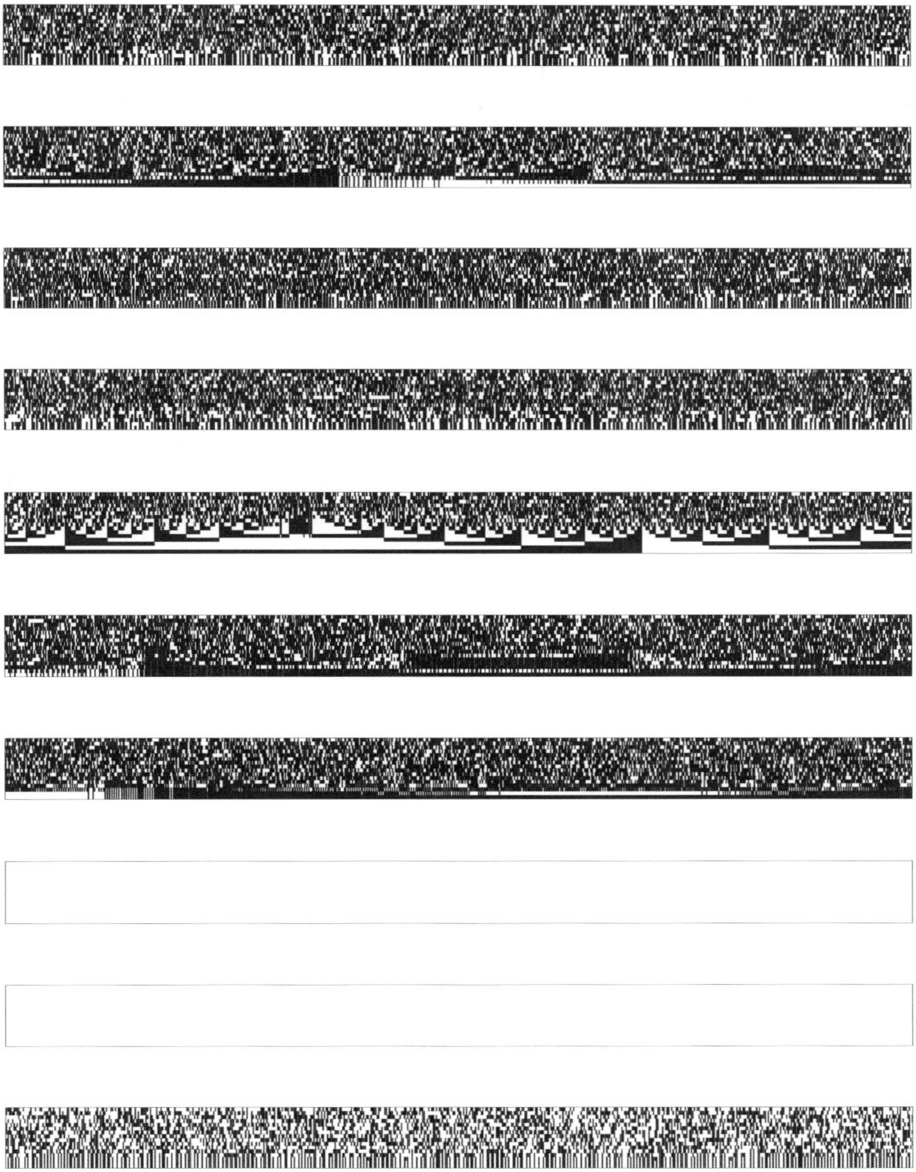

dataphonic 10 structure 03:00 - 06:00 left

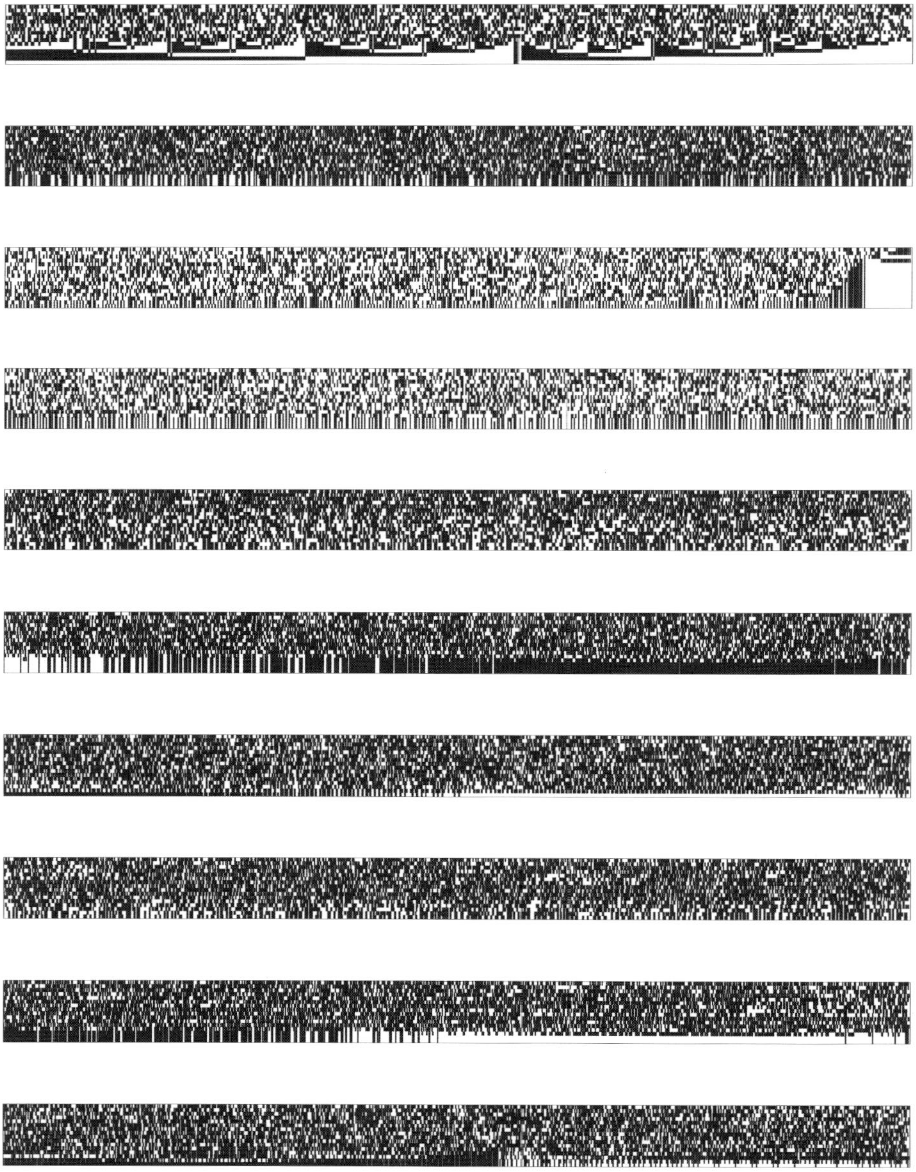

dataphonics 10 structure 03:00 - 06:00 right

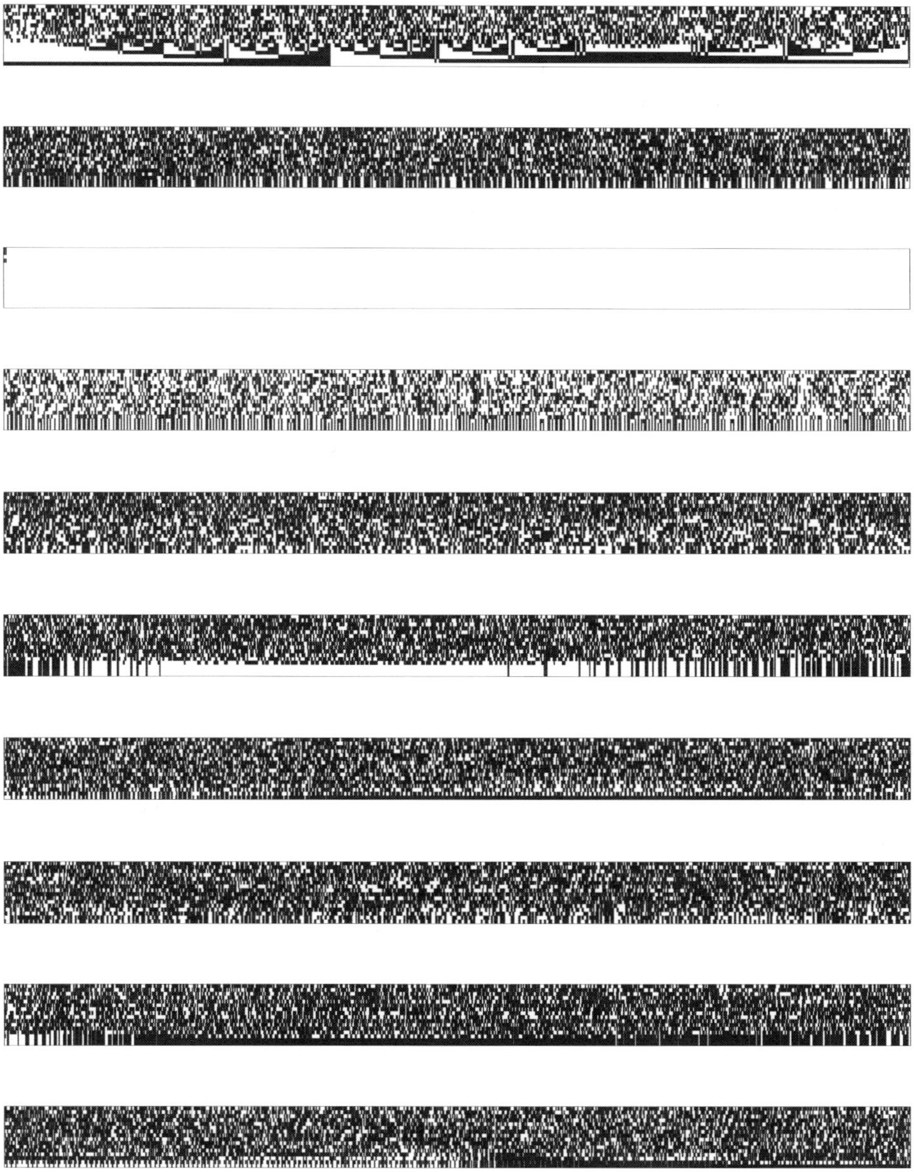